The Journals
#TWO   Trilogy

VENGEANCE

BY

D.M. EARL

COPYRIGHT

Copyright @ 2015 D.M. Earl
Published by D.M. Earl
ISBN 13: 978-0692595541
ISBN 10: 0692595546

For any questions or comments please email the author directly at dmearl14@gmail.com

This book is a work of fiction. All characters, events and places portrayed

WARNING

Due to content this book is intended for mature audiences only (18+) and contains explicit descriptions of violence, torture and intense sexual situations including rape. Also included are severe mind games.
The subjects in this book could cause triggers in some so please take this warning seriously.
If any of these subjects affect you in any way I suggest this book is not for you.

TABLE OF CONTENT

ACKNOWLEDGEMENTS

Margreet Asselbergs, my Illustrator who I am blessed to also call my friend. Margreet has a talent like no other. No matter what I ask of her she always finds a way to manage my requests. The end designs are phenomenal and way beyond what I could even imagined.

Thank you Margreet for your mad ass talent and more importantly for your continued support of my work and dreams. I couldn't do it without you.

Dana Hook, my Editor whose ability to see where I want my books to go, who seems to read my mind even if I can't get the sentence or direction exactly right. Dana is someone I admire immensely. She puts her heart into everything she does. Sometimes she goes to the extreme. Dana is a wonderful woman I am proud to call my editor and friend. With her on my team never worry about the finished product, as she will make it perfect.

Katie Harder-Schauer, my Proofreader who takes such care and time with my words to make sure they are perfect. I can't thank you enough Katie. I appreciate your skill and diligence with the English language. You are the final person to touch my story checking to make sure everything is awesome.

Beta Readers, my lifesavers. Laura, Karen and Chris I appreciate you girls more than you will ever know. Your honesty sometimes guts me but also makes me a better writer. Sending my proofs to you allows me an insight to see what readers really want. Also I get an in depth look at how a reader would view my books. I appreciate the time and care you take with my books. But more importantly I am grateful for your friendships. I look forward to many years of friendship and interaction.

Fellow Authors who have helped me with a kind word, direction and advice. I am honored to know such wonderful women and call each and every one of you my friends. Thank you for all you have shared and guided me with.

Bloggers, without all of you I would still be struggling on how to get my name out there. The dedication each of you has for authors is awe-inspiring. I am honored to know each of you and so appreciate all you do for me.

DEDICATIONS

Chuck (The Duke of Earl)-Husband extraordinaire who has continually supported me as I pursue my dream of writing. Thank you baby for picking up the slack while I sit at my desk. I probably don't say it enough but I truly appreciate all you do. I really do. Darlin love ya heart and soul.

My girls-Freya, Brook, Jaci, Dana, Shirley, Stephanie, Keri, Christine and Karen. For always being there for me and making me laugh so hard my tummy hurts. Each of you are so very special to me for what ya share and who you are. Blessed to have met ya and call you my sista's.

My PA's- Laura and Shanean all I can say is thank you for all you both do. My life has been made easier with each of you in it.

No words can express how much you both mean to me. You allow me to do what I love which is writing.

D.M.'s Horde-Ladies I can't thank you enough for all of your support. The daily interaction keeps me grounded knowing Ya'll have my back no matter what. Our weekly book reviews and get togethers have become my favorite night. Getting to know each of you has been the best highlight. Your love of reading brings such joy to my life. Thanks for your continued loyalty, shares, posts, messages and just being there for me always. Ya'll mean so much to me.

Authors-To all who have opened their hearts and minds to me when I asked question on top of question. Your friendships mean the world to me. Your openness and willingness to share and help has been phenomenal. Thanks for allowing me into the world of writing. There are way too many to name but know how much Ya'll truly mean to me. I have been blessed that no matter whom or when I have contacted you always have been kind and generous. Your help is much appreciated.

Readers-You AMAZE me with your constant support and outpouring of love. I am blown away by your dedication to authors (this one in particular) and your love of reading. Because of such love I get to do what I love, write. So a humbled *thank you* to each and every reader. Thanks for your love of books.

PROLOGUE

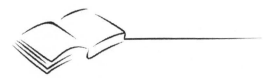

Following behind Stone, watching his sports car weave in and out of traffic as I try to keep up with him in my Jeep, I go over what the fuck has happened so far: Walker approaching me, Stone showing his hand at my house.

Stone.

Just his name sends shivers down my spine and I can't convince myself if it's a good or bad thing.

All these years, through my dreams and nightmares, those damn green eyes have been a constant, and now that I've finally met the man, I'm more confused than ever. On one hand, I want to put a bullet between those eyes for just watching and not helping me. But after hearing his side, I do sort of understand why. He thought someone was coming. How could he know that that help would never arrive? Nevertheless, it doesn't make me any less pissed off at him. So, with everything going on, what the fuck do I do? I have a masturbation session with a stranger and have one of the best orgasms I've had in a very long time.

Barely making the lane switch and left turn has me wondering why he's driving like a lunatic. Engaging my navigation—thankful we had exchanged numbers—I tell my phone stud to dial Stone's cell. Listening to the ringing in my Jeep, I wait for him to pick up the call.

"Hey babe, what's up? Havin' a hard time keeping up with me?" he laughs.

"Not having a hard time. You drive like a fucking maniac, Stone. What's the rush?" Before I give him a chance to respond, I continue, "I just called to let you know that if I lose you, I'll meet you at Sweet Bits & Pieces. I'm not going to kill myself because you have a need for speed in that machine you're in."

Hearing his reply of "whatever" before I disconnect, I decrease my speed to the speed limit and watch him disappear from my sight.

Fuck, fuck, fuck!

What am I supposed to do? For the last ten years I've wanted nothing more than to get vengeance on the assholes that ruined my family's and my lives. Thinking back on my first few blue journals, I knew I was almost to the point of insanity with the things I wrote down; the types of tortures I would bring down upon them. There were so many slow and painful ways I wanted to make them all suffer. I thought of slowly gutting them, maybe even removing their fingers and toes with rusty bolt cutters. Also removing other appendages, such as castration. My mind was all over the place and putting those thoughts down on paper helped me to get out my anger and intense pain.

Over the years, my torture schemes went from physical to emotional, then finally to psychological. Mind fucking began to feel like the ultimate revenge in the end. I remember having dreams of them not only losing everything important in their lives, but forcing them to do the ultimate act— pushing them into such darkness as to commit suicide.

Never did I truly believe that I would be given the opportunity to do it. With the information Stone provided last night, I now know that only five are left, and that includes Walker.

Taking a deep breath, I ask myself the real question. Could I actually go through with their ruin or torture ... eventually their deaths? To comprehend what I'm even considering gives me goose bumps, but the bigger question is once it is done, will I be able to live with myself.

I stop at a red light and take a second to let my mind wander when suddenly I hear a horn blow, right before my Jeep is pushed forward. Some asshole just hit me from behind.

I glance in my rearview mirror and see the face glaring back at me. My body starts to shake as my breath catches in my throat. It can't be *him*.

Motherfucker. How were he and Walker able to locate me after all these years?

It's the giant man from that night, so many years ago. He looks the same, but older ... scarier, and he's staring me down through my mirror with a smirk on his face.

Looking around, I can't believe how we're the only two cars at the light. He reverses and I look ahead at the cross traffic, trying to find a hole so I can run through the red light without hitting anyone, but there's no way for me to make it through. He rams into my Jeep again, forcing me closer into the intersection.

Trying not to panic, I hit my navigation, instructing it to dial Stone. As I wait for him to answer, I hear the sound of tires screeching behind me, drawing my attention to not only the giant in his huge SUV, but also—*"Son-of-a-bitch!"* I scream as I see Walker in a black on black Range Rover, pulling up directly behind the SUV that's trying to launch me into oncoming traffic.

"What's up, Quinn? Did ya get lost?"

"Stone, I have a bit of a problem."

As I try to explain the situation, the light changes and I floor it, trying to get away from the disaster about to happen. The two men behind me are determined to hurt me ... again.

"What's wrong, Quinn? Talk to me." I hear him yell to someone, "Johnny, get your ass in here now. We have a problem."

"I have unwanted company following me. It's Walker and one of the guys from that night. They had me trapped at a red light. I'm finally on the move again, but they're tailing me. My Jeep doesn't stand a chance at getting away from them. What do I do? I don't want to lead them to the bakery with people there, so tell me what to do." I'm starting to scream now.

"Tell me where you are exactly." I can hear him and someone else running, then hear car doors slamming shut in the background.

"Just coming up to North Ave, about five minutes away."

"Keep driving this way. I'm back on the road, heading in your direction. Don't do anything stupid, Quinn. Remember, they're dangerous."

Really? Is he stupid? I *know* they're fucking dangerous. I'm the one who can testify to that shit personally. Nevertheless, I try to keep calm as I watch them stay close behind me.

Besides Walker, that big asshole was the worst that night. He made sure that I knew how much he got off on my pain and humiliation. Just as much as Walker, I'm still trying to recover from his type of brutality. He was horrible. I still wake from nightmares from his type of torture.

Before I make a right turn that would bring me to the street my business is on, I see the Range Rover in the wrong lane of traffic, trying to get in front of me. Just as he goes to cut me off I make the turn on a red light, not even caring at this point. I will never let myself be at their mercy again.

Just as I'm straightening out the Jeep from the turn, I see an extended cab pickup truck heading my way with someone waving his or her arms in the passenger seat. I see its Stone with someone else driving.

Steering the Jeep sharply to the left and into the oncoming lane, which thank God is empty, allows their pickup to pass me just as the giant is turning onto the street.   The guy driving with Stone has a crazy ass smile on his face as I hear the engine roar past me as he floors the vehicle right at the giant in the SUV. I feel like I'm watching an action movie.

Seeing this, the giant tries to move out of their way by going into the other lane and plows right into the rear passenger door of Walker's Rover. The sound of crushing metal is loud, as neither man decreased their speed. Stone and his crazy friend end up further clipping the SUV, pushing him into a spin as Walker flies by and gets away.

When the SUV finally comes to a stop, facing the wrong way, both Stone and crazy dude jump out of their truck, dragging him out of his vehicle and throwing him to the ground as the crazy dude proceeds to stomp on him before Stone is able to pull him away. This all happens right in front of me in a matter of minutes and a few blinks of an eye. Christ, does it ever end?

Stone approaches me cautiously, his eyes on me the entire time. "You okay, Quinn?"

Nodding, I quietly say, "Yeah, I think so."

"He's one of them, isn't he ... one of the five?" I nod again. "Well, didn't think it would happen so quickly, but you need to decide what you want to do with him. We'll follow your lead but we need to make it quick. It's only a matter of time before the police show up, so what's it going to be; let him go, kill him, or pack him up and handle it later? I need your answer, sugar."

Well, I guess the time has come for me to finally put my big girl panties on and face my past head-on, here in the present.

CHAPTER 1

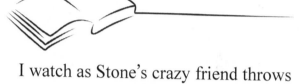

I watch as Stone's crazy friend throws cuffs on the semiconscious giant and with little effort, helps the man up and walks him to the truck, throwing the giant in the back of the crew cab. Glancing back at Stone, I feel suddenly scared and confused.

Holy shit.

What am I doing? I have two kids and two sisters to worry about. Not to mention the bakery, Ivy, and my employees, who depend on me for their livelihood?

Jumping down from my Jeep, I approach Stone and he reaches for me, pulling me into his side. "We'll put him up at one of the safe houses until you make a decision on what you want to do with him. This actually works to our advantage because it leaves Walker with one less stooge."

His words bring an unexpected giggle bursting from my lips as I throw my hands over my mouth. But then I ask, "What happens if I decide I can't do anything to them? Will you let him go?"

"Sugar, I can promise you that he will never hurt another woman. Worst-case scenario, he'll spend his days in jail being somebody's bitch. He won't like it, but that's just too fucking bad. Don't you worry, we'll figure this out. Now, let's get to the bakery and talk to Ivy. I'm gonna make a quick call so one of my guys can come and get this beast of an SUV out of here and make it disappear. I'll follow you and Johnny here can fall in behind me. You okay with that?"

Taking a deep breath, I look into those emerald green eyes that have haunted me for years and nod my head.

"Yeah, I'm good."

Ivy's mouth is hanging wide open as we walk down the hall to my office. Her eyes are going from Stone to Johnny, then back to Stone. I hide my grin as she finally looks at me, confusion all over her face.

"Quinn, uh, who are these guys?"

I hear both men snicker as I open the door to my office. The look on Johnny's face as he looks at Ivy is scary. He looks downright lethal. Watching her walk past him, his eyes take in her long blonde hair that touches the top her heart-shaped ass. I can almost feel the heat of his stare.

Turning my attention to Stone, I catch him crack Johnny in the back of his head. "What the fuck, dude ... really?"

Stone gives him a dangerous glare, which in turn, shuts Johnny up before he can even breathe a word.

"Boys, let's try and get along. There is a lot that needs to be handled so no pissing in the sandbox, okay?" Stone smiles while Johnny pouts.

I walk to the sofa, taking a seat next to Ivy who is silently watching everyone, taking everything in. Both Stone and Johnny pull the chairs from my desk to sit in front of us.

"Ivy, this is Stone and Johnny. Guys, this is Ivy."

Stone gives her a chin lift, while Johnny stands to shake her hand. "It's a pleasure to meet ya, Ivy." As she reaches to shake his hand, he raises it to his lips and kisses the top, never taking his eyes from hers. Ivy gasps. The sexual tension between the two is so thick that I could cut it with one of my bakery knives.

Clearing my throat, Johnny winks at Ivy before sitting back down. "You done? We got to get this shit done so Quinn can go see her family," Stone says. Johnny glares at Stone before giving him a brief nod. Stone looks my way and smiles before turning to Ivy.

"Ivy, I know Quinn shared with you the events that occurred ten years ago, including her journey since that time. I know you're her friend so we have a favor to ask of you. Quinn's in danger, and that's why we're here, to protect her."

Ivy immediately glances at me with a knowing look in her eyes. "Yeah, it's Walker. Not only has he found me again, he's now stalking me, along with a friend of his from that night. I'm thinking they want me dead."

"That explains a lot. This morning when I got here there was garbage all over the back and someone had thrown dog shit on all the windows. It was disgusting. I took a picture so we could show you."

Gross. However, I reach for her phone. She pulls up the camera app and hits the screen a couple of times before handing it over to me. Yep, I'm immediately grossed out as I enlarge the picture so both Stone and Johnny can see it too.

This was no accident. The entire front window was smeared with what appeared to be some form of feces. What a fucking sight to see for a food service business. Thank

God Ivy always arrives way before we open for the day.

"Did you by chance call the cops, Ivy ... make a report?" Stone inquires.

Shaking her head, Ivy lowers her eyes before replying. "No, didn't even think about it. I just wanted to get that shit off the windows before customers started coming in. We have a lot of regulars early in the mornings and I didn't want them to see that. Sorry."

"Honey, don't apologize. It's not a problem."

At Stone's words, we all hear a vicious growl and turn to see Johnny glaring at Stone. Stone returns the look then laughs. "Dude, calm the fuck down. I got my hands full with that one..." he says as he points at me, "and don't need any more trouble. We good?"

Johnny looks to Stone with an evil grin. "Oh yeah, we're good."

Stone shakes his head and continues on with his explanation as to why we're at the bakery. "So, Ivy, as you know, Walker's found Quinn and unfortunately, his intentions aren't good. Between me and my crew, we're going to protect Quinn and her family, so we're gonna need to switch up the schedule here, and we need your help."

As he goes through our plan, Ivy sits quietly, listening to his every word, with an occasional glance at me. I can tell she's dying to ask me a ton of questions regarding what the hell is going on with these two. I finally give her an opening.

"Ivy, what's up? Talk to me, sweetie."

"Quinn, I've gotta ask because after what you told me yesterday, it's scary to think what I'm thinking, but..." She motions towards Stone and leans toward me, trying to whisper, which she can't do to save her life, "is he your green-eyed guy from that night?"

"Yes, Stone is that green-eyed guy. Now, before you freak the fuck out, let me explain." I tell her how Stone came back into my life and how he's had his crew watching over me all these years. Her eyes couldn't possibly get any larger as I explain the journals I've kept over the years. When it dawns on her what the blue journals represent, her bottom lip starts to tremble as she runs her hands up and down her arms, rocking back and forth. I know my friend is extremely educated and has put two and two together, figuring out what I'm planning to do. Just as I begin to say something to calm her, the door to my office is thrown open as one of the biggest men I have ever seen in my life enters, immediately catching Stone's eye.

"The asshole is waking up in the back of the truck. What do you want me do? I can knock him out, use the chloroform, or we can shoot him the fuck up and keep him out for hours."

Realizing that he's speaking freely in front of both Ivy and myself, I watch his eyes narrow and his entire body tenses up.

"They good Boss, or do we need to adjust our plan? I got room for a couple more if needed."

I immediately pull Ivy closer to me as Stone stands and approaches the guy, speaking quietly to him. As he listens, I can tell they're talking about me as he looks my way and gives me one of the gentlest smiles I have ever seen on a man's face. He nods at me then looks to Ivy, and I mean really looks at her, and licks his lips. Johnny immediately moves to sit on the other side of her. He may as well piss on her and mark her as his territory. Stone is taking all of this in and finally decides to speak.

"Quinn, Ivy, this big lug is Diesel, and he's part of my crew. Don't let his size scare you away. He's normally a gentle teddy bear." He then looks to Diesel. "Do whatever you have to do to keep that asshole asleep. I'll leave that to you."

With an evil smirk, Diesel starts to head out, but he stops and turns abruptly. "Ladies, nice to meet ya. You need anything, they know how to get a hold of me."

Then he turns and he's gone.

After discussing the plan for the bakery with Ivy, both Stone and I stay in my office as I take care of some business. Johnny follows Ivy out like a puppy following their owner. With Stone on his phone, I take the time to use the facilities before heading out to the safe house.

When entering the bathroom, I get the strangest feeling. Something is off, but I can't put my finger on it. Going to the toilet, I notice the lid is down. That's strange because no one, not even the cleaning crew, ever puts the top lid down. Once I lift the lid, I see a smear of something red. Hands shaking, I step back as my breath catches in my throat. Glancing around the single bathroom I notice the garbage can filled with crumpled up paper towels, with what looks to be blood.

I scream for Stone and the door flies open with both Stone and Johnny running in. I point to the toilet and Stone steps up, shoving me into Johnny's arms, who proceeds to turn me away. I hear the lid hit the back of the tank and Stone says, "Motherfucker." Trying to turn, Johnny holds tight as Stone tells him to get me out now.

I push back against Johnny and I pinch his side as hard as I can. Immediately his hands release me and I turn quickly, managing to see Stone as he pulls out what looks like a stuffed animal of some sort, but then it dawns on me. Fuck, it isn't a stuffed animal at all. It's a tortured baby kitten. Someone had cut chunks out of the poor thing, but what catches my eye is the brand burned into the poor kitten's stomach. Oh my God, that son-of-a-bitch.

It's there, as clear as day, the same fucking W that Walker put on my inner thigh. He was here in my personal space, letting me know he can get to me whenever he wants to.

I'm totally fucked, and I suddenly start to feel nauseous and dizzy. As I reach for something to hold me up, I hear both Stone and Johnny calling my name, but I'm already on my way to the darkness that's pulling me under.

CHAPTER 2

Slowly coming to, I feel something cool and wet on my forehead and   hear people whispering around me. Rubbing my hands down my face, the whispering stops as I hear Stone softly call my name.

"I'm awake, Stone. He was here, wasn't he? How the fuck did he get in here with that fucking state-of-the-art alarm system that I had installed? I'm not safe anywhere am I? He's going to get to me and there's nothing anyone can do."

Gently pulling me to him, I'm enveloped in his warmth as his lips press into my forehead.

"Sugar, I'm tellin' ya, we got your back. He's playing on your emotions and insecurities. Don't let him in there. Fight back because if you really want your revenge, you've gotta toughen up. Walker is going to be pulling out the big guns so you need to prepare yourself, Quinn. Not to mention, we need to decide what we're going to do with the remaining five men. We've got one right now, probably bleeding and drugged by Diesel as he sits in the truck listening to music, drinking a pop and keeping watch."

Looking up into those emerald eyes, I feel his words wash over me as we stare at each other, letting the rest of the world fall away. His eyes take me back to my past for a split second, then immediately back to the present when he gives me a gentle squeeze. I take in his unique scent, which is fresh, clean, and slightly musky. His body is wrapped around me, protecting me from harm while his presence calms me and clears my head of the thoughts fighting to take over.

A clearing of someone's throat has me looking over his shoulder to see both Ivy and Johnny watching us intently. I try pulling myself away from his arms, but he maintains an ironclad grip around me.

"You okay, Quinn? I heard you scream and ran back, only to have Johnny here tell me to stay put before Stone came out carrying you, demanding cold compresses. What the heck happened?"

"Ivy, have you been in the bathroom today?"

"No. I started filling the displays as soon as I cleaned the windows. Why?"

Stone releases me, letting me sit up on the couch while he goes to the fridge, grabbing a cold water and bringing it back to me, motioning for me to drink up.

He looks towards the couple standing by the door, waiting for a response. "Walker, or one of his henchmen, were here and left a present for Quinn in the bathroom. It freaked her the fuck out, and that's what happened. Johnny, go check out the security video and let me know what you find."

Giving Ivy a quick squeeze, he rushes past her. Ivy walks farther into the room and sits next me, pulling me into her arms. I can feel her fear as we both sit there huddled together while Stone goes through the protocol we're going to follow going forward. He stops for a minute to call someone, explaining the system needs to be updated immediately. Whomever he's speaking to must have finished because Stone disconnects the call.

"Okay, we got that straight. From now on, one of my guys will be here at Sweet Bits & Pieces to make sure this doesn't happen again. Now that we have everything out there and both you and Ivy have a schedule that works for everyone, you ready to go Quinn? We need to get to the house so you can see your—*humph*. What the fuck was that for?"

Giving Stone the stink eye, I look from him to Ivy and back to him again. It takes a moment, but then he gets it. Ivy doesn't know about the twins. Guess it's time to tell her my final secret. *Shit.* This is going to be hard.

Watching my face, Stone walks to the door, looking over his shoulder. "Gonna go check on our friend in the truck with Diesel. Be back in a few."

Thankful for his exit, I look at my friend whom, for some reason, I never told about the twins. At times I felt she would look at me differently and I didn't want to chance it, so I kept my personal and business life separate. Ivy knows about my sisters, I just didn't tell her about Cari and Benjamin, but the time is here.

"Ivy, I have one more thing to tell you. I want you to listen to me before you say anything, ok?"

She nods.

"Shit, this is so fucking hard for so many reasons, Ivy. Yesterday, one of my deepest secrets came out and I explained to you what happened over ten years ago: the death of my parents, my brutal rape that led to my hiding out for all these years. I left one thing out, and please don't be mad when I tell you. This secret was to keep people safe from Walker. After the rape, I was taken to the hospital and assumed since they knew I was raped, that they would have done what was necessary to protect me. Well, about a month after the rape, I was feeling pretty shitty and couldn't keep anything in my stomach. My sister, Raven, suggested a pregnancy test, and needless to say, it came back positive. I was pregnant by one of my rapists."

Hearing her gasp, I can't bring myself to look at her as I continue. "At first I was adamant about having an abortion. How the fuck could I raise a child that was conceived in such a horrific manner? How could I look at that child every day, a constant reminder of what I went through? My younger sister, Viola, sat me down and gave me shit. She's wise beyond her years. She explained to me that no matter what, an innocent child who never asked to be brought into this world out of a vile act, was growing inside of me. She insisted I go see an OB-GYN. She even went with me. Ivy, let me tell you that the first time I heard the heartbeat, I felt like my life was finally starting. That sound, which reminded me of waves at the beach, cleared my head and I decided to keep it. Women did it every day, so how hard could it be? While both Viola and I were listening to the most beautiful sound in the world, my baby, the technician seemed to have an issue with the machine. Running the wand back and forth over my stomach, she smiled widely and looked at both of us and rocked my world when she said, "Quinn, great news. You're having twins."

That almost put me over the edge. Two babies would mean two of everything. Once I was done, we went back home and I had a serious conversation with both Viola and Raven. There was no way I could keep the kids safe. Walker was still loose and had connections all over. Even though he went silent, that didn't mean he wasn't watching. So, between the three of us, we figured out the best thing to do was for them to take the twins and move away. We bought a ranch in the country and that's where they've been all this time. I go out on weekends and whenever I take time off as to spend it with my children. They are my life Ivy."

Taking a deep breath, I raise my eyes to see hers filled with tears. She pulls me to her and holds me tightly as she starts to bawl. Why is *she* fucking crying?

"Ivy, damn it. Ivy, what's the matter?"

She wipes her running nose on my sleeve ... *Really?*

"Holy crap, Quinn. You're a momma? I can't believe this, and I'm kind of pissed you didn't think you could trust me with it. But as long as they are safe, that's all that matters. Does Stone know about them?"

Nodding, I proceed to finish the story. "Stone knows everything. He's been watching me, or I should say him and his crew have kept a close watch on my sisters, the twins, and me. That alone freaks me the fuck out, but no one has ever harmed any of us, so I won't overreact."

She's watching me closely, so I wait because I know what's coming.

"Quinn, do you have any idea who the children's father might be?" I know she doesn't mean to hurt me, but her question does. Just like every other time someone asked, or even when the twins wanted to know.

"I have an idea, but never did any testing because to me, that person is just a sperm donor. They are my kids Ivy make no mistake. I would die for them in a second, absolutely no hesitation."

"I'm hurt that you didn't trust me enough to tell me, but I get it, I really do. It's going to take me some time to absorb all that you've shared with me, but I would love to meet the kids someday if that's okay? Kind of late I guess, but congratulations, sweetie. I am so proud of you and damn glad to have you in my life."

Her hug is genuine, like she always is with me. Knowing I owe her for so much, I continue to share.

"Ivy, any one of them could be the father, but the physician told me that both my kids are from the same man. I didn't even know that it was possible to get pregnant by two different men. Anyway, after the twins were born and as they grew, I could see some of their father in them;

especially in their eyes, but I also knew I would never share that with him if I could find him. He would take my kids away from me in a second.

"Please tell me they aren't Walker's?"

"No! No, thank God, they aren't his. They look just like his right hand man who goes by the name of Dirk. From what Stone's told me, there are only five of the men left. Walker's either killed or removed all the others and kept only the men totally loyal to him. So, now that this shit is coming to the surface, I have to make sure they don't see the twins because they'll see it, and I'll not lose my kids to those psycho's."

As Ivy and I talk about Cari and Benjamin and all that has transpired in our lives in a short period of time, I feel deep inside like this is the first chapter of something truly evil about to enter our lives.

CHAPTER 3

After spending most of the morning and early afternoon with Ivy, going over everything, we finally head out. I'm not sure where we're going, but Stone and his guys know our next stop.

It's kind of weird getting in the pickup truck and looking over the seat to see the giant laying on his side, face badly bruised, still in cuffs with a piece of duct tape across his mouth. His breathing is even at least. Looking at him, I'm so confused. A small part of me feels really bad, but the larger part feels he deserves whatever he receives. Remembering how cruel he was and how he had no regard for me as a human being hardens my heart towards him.

I watch his eyes begin to open slowly. He must have felt my stare because he opens his eyes and tilts his head until he can focus on me. I see the exact moment he recognizes me as his pupils dilate even further than they already are. His breathing starts to quicken as we glare at each other. Not sure what to do, I turn my head and look for one of the guys, then I hear a noise from where the giant is lying. Not wanting to give him the satisfaction of having any more of my attention, I yell out, "Hey, this asshole's awake. What do you want me to do with him?"

Johnny and Diesel immediately approach the vehicle, rounding towards the back end. Opening the doors, Diesel immediately pulls back and punches the giant in the kidney area of his back. The giant's eyes close in pain for just a moment, and then they shoot back open, full of anger.

Johnny reaches into the vehicle and grabs a small black pouch. He pulls out a syringe and a bottle of something—I have no idea what it is—and proceeds to fill the syringe with the liquid before going back and plunging the needle into the giant's muscle.

I watch as his eyes roll back and shut as his body relaxes immediately. Johnny quickly finishes putting everything back into the pouch and closes the cargo door.

I'm watching so intently that I don't hear Stone coming up beside me until his arm reaches to pull me in. I turn and punch him in the gut.

"Shit, Quinn, what the fuck was that for? Damn, that hurt. Where did you learn to punch like that?"

"Don't assume you can touch me whenever you want to Stone. I don't like anyone in my space, got it?"

He stands there, hand on his gut and his eyes on me. It's intense. Nodding, he motions for me to get in the truck as he tells Diesel to meet us at the safe house.

Looking around, Johnny waits for me to get in before he jumps in the back, sitting the giant up in the seat before taking the seat next to him. As Stone starts to drive away from Sweet Bits & Pieces, I feel like what's coming next is going to be a huge fucking life changer.

I must have dozed off because the rough road wakes me from my deep sleep. As the fog leaves my head, I can hear both Johnny and Stone speaking about the next steps and what to do with the giant.

"Man, you know she isn't gonna be able to pull this off. No matter how bad that night was, Quinn isn't capable of torture and murder. We need to get our shit together before Walker catches us with our pants down. Also, gotta get that laptop from her and back to headquarters where it'll be safe 'cause we all know that if they get their hands on it first, we're all so fuckin' screwed."

"Johnny, you think I don't know that? Shit, this is moving way too fast, and you might be right about her not being able to do what needs to be done. But that's why we're here, to make sure it ends no matter what. Ten years is long enough. Quinn and her family deserve to be able to live their lives to the fullest without fear. If she decides to let us put these assholes away for life, that's what'll happen. But the decision is Quinn's and no matter what, whatever she wants done to them, we *will* do it. You know how I feel about the whole torture shit, but since that night I've wanted to get my hands on each and every one of these motherfuckers. You didn't see what they did to her. That piece of shit beside you was almost as bad as Walker. He tortured Quinn and showed her absolutely no mercy. So, if torture is what she wants, that's what she's gonna get. Call ahead and let Spirit know we're on the way with a package. Tell her to get the shed ready."

Listening to Johnny speak to this "Spirit," I'm shocked to hear a woman's voice on the other end. Holy shit. Who are these people and how can a woman be a part of Stone's crew? He explained to me that they were ghosts for the government and worked undercover all over the world, handling situations that needed their expertise. What the hell could her skill set be? My curiosity is piqued.

Stretching, I can feel Stone's eyes on me. I look just in time to see his eyes take me in, stopping at my breasts, and then going down my slightly curved belly to land on my legs. Bringing his eyes to me, I'm shocked to see lust he's barely containing in them. I start to feel the same feelings I felt last night, but I push them back because my feelings for this man are all over the place. One feeling I still have is anger from the past and even though I had a weak moment last night, having that stupid fucking masturbation session with him, I'm not ready to let that happen again anytime soon. I need to put some space between us so instead of acknowledging his look, I turn and stare out the window.

As we approach what looks to be an old factory of some sort, Stone pulls up to the gate. We don't wait long before the gate slowly starts to open. We drive down a long, curved driveway where trees are lined up on either side of the road. As we approach, I'm able to make out multiple buildings in a semicircle. There are lights on in the largest building, both on the first and second floor. The closer we get, the more I can make out of the building. It appears to be some sort of hanger I think. There's also a pole barn and a large shed to the side of the main building.

Pulling up in front of the largest building, Stone shuts the car off and turns to me.

"Quinn we need to be very careful with your sister Raven until we know why she's maintained contact with Walker. I know she's your blood, but we have to put you and the kid's safety as priority. So I don't want you alone with her, and try not to leave Cari or Benjamin alone with her. My guys have been able to keep her occupied with getting this place in order, but I don't have a good feeling about her part in all this, and I always follow my gut."

Not sure what to say, I nod. "Okay. Now, it's time for you to let me know what your plan is. We need to figure out what we're doing with Kenny here." As my head shoots up, he smirks. "Sugar, there's nothing I don't know about Walker and his guys. I've had ten years to get in their heads and believe me; I'm firmly there. So, what's it gonna be Quinn? Do we handle this here, or do you want him to spend his life in prison. The choice is yours."

Finding myself at this crossroad, I take a moment to give this some serious thought. Knowing Walker the way I do, or did, I just know that if we put Kenny the giant in jail, he will have him killed to keep him quiet. So, how much would he really suffer? But on the other hand, can I torture and kill him? I mean really, I'm a baker and mother of two. Do I really have it in me to do it?

Remembering what I've written in my vengeance journals over the years, I realize it was so much easier to write my thoughts of anger down than ever truly *do* any of that crazy shit. It was all talk. I never once thought I'd be given an opportunity to do any of it. If I decide I want him dead, Stone and his people can handle it, but is that fair to them? I don't know what to do, and I know everyone is waiting on my answer.

I look to Stone. He's patiently waiting with no expression on his face, waiting for me to play God; to make the decision to end someone's life. That's when I have a flashback of what my parents had went through, all because they loved Walker. No one worried about ending their lives or torturing them. This asshole, Kenny, was one of many who actually beat my father to death.

Closing my eyes, I say a quiet prayer, asking both God and my parents' to forgive me for the road I'm about to take. Knowing it's not right; I make a decision from the heart.

"I want that slime bag to suffer for his part in my parents' death and my rape. Do what needs to be done, but I want him to suffer and know that it was me that decided his fate. I want him dead."

CHAPTER 4

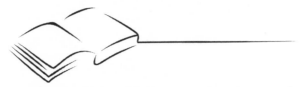

Watching the scene unfold in front of me, I begin to doubt my decision. As soon as I gave Stone my answer, he flashed his lights and two people came out of the building. One was definitely a woman; I could tell by her shape. When they got closer to the vehicle, I looked at both of them. The man was scary. He looked to have had burn scars. Seeing me stare, he gave me a chin lift and a small smile. The woman on the other hand, had the most discerning eyes I'd ever seen. Her eyes were such a pale blue; I thought they almost looked white with dark pupils. But what scared me was the empty look they held. She had dead eyes, and when she glanced my way, I felt a shiver run down my spine. Nothing else, just a glance, and then she moved to the cargo area that held the giant, Kenny.

Following them, I hear Stone tell them what I want. At that, the woman turns to me and gives me an eerie grin. That freaks me out, but I don't want to appear weak, so I put my hands in my pockets and wait. I look at them all and try to figure out how they all fit together. Johnny, Diesel, and Stone, lift Kenny out of the back and walk to the shed, left of the main building.

Entering the shed, I know what I'm looking at. I've been in something similar to this before. This is their torture room. So many items are laid out on tables and trays.

Feeling like I'm falling back in time, I put my hand to the wall for some support. With Stone's hands full of Kenny, he shouts, "Spirit, get a goddamn chair over to Quinn before she hits the fuckin' floor for Christ's sake."

The woman who I now know is Spirit, grabs a chair on wheels and flings it my way where it bangs into the wall. I grab for it and sit, putting my head between my legs as I try to catch my breath.

"Girl, you need to pull your shit together." Hearing the softest voice with a hint of southern twang, I look up to see Spirit crouched in front of me. Up close I can see her eyes are actually a light violet blue, rimmed in black. "I can't imagine what you're going through, but know we all have your back. Nothing is gonna happen that you don't want to, okay? Just remember what these assholes did to you and your family. Because of them, you lost time with your parents. You lost precious time with your sisters. Those kids have had to live isolated for their own good. Then remember what they did to you. Not one of them tried to stop the events of that day. Each one of them was worse than the next. This asshole did all that sick shit to you with no regards to you as a human being. Now, think about all that thought you put into your journals."

My eyes widen at the fact she even knows about my journals.

"Sorry, Quinn, I've read them. Actually, we all have, but before you get pissed, we needed to know what we were dealing with. We were each assigned a color to study and analyze. I was impressed with your later books on revenge, once you realized that your earlier journals were emotional and outrageous. Some of your torture ideas impressed me and girl, I'll tell you that that takes a lot. So, take a deep breath, and if you can't handle this, go outside. We're only going to secure Kenny and give him something to think on."

Watching her turn, I realize that she's the team's torture expert. *Holy shit*. This woman is the one who carries out the interrogations with pain and torture.

I lean back in my chair, pushing it against the wall. My eyes are wide and fearful. I take in their practiced dance as they lean an unconscious Kenny against the hospital bed so they can remove his clothes, leaving him in only his briefs. Johnny and Diesel toss him on the bed covered in plastic. This isn't their first rodeo.

Restraints are pulled from under the bed and tightened to keep him in place. So absorbed in what the men are doing, I lose track of Spirit. As she enters my view, I'm shocked to see her pushing a tray toward the bed. She has on what looks to be a butcher's apron and gloves. Her long black hair is pulled back and tucked into a tight bun on the top of her head. She has safety glasses on and the look in her eyes is scary as hell.

She reaches for a syringe with a long needle and pushes it into Kenny's chest, right by his heart. Immediately his eyes open as he struggles to take a deep breath. Seeing that the tape on his mouth is preventing him from getting that breath, Spirit grabs a corner of the tape as he stares at her with pleading eyes. Without even blinking, she rips the tape from his lips, taking some of the skin with it from his upper lip. He lets out a painful groan before taking in a huge gulp of air.

Reaching for a cup of something on the table, Spirit puts a straw in it and brings it to Kenny's lips. He watches her cautiously, but you can tell he wants to take a drink. His mouth has to be so dry from hours of sitting in the pickup truck and the drugs they were shooting into him. Before he takes a sip, Spirit leans over him, her lips almost touching his ear.

"Motherfucker, you puke this up, I'll make you regret it, so just drink it down and suck it up. Got it?"

Immediately he tries to pull back, but Johnny comes around, holding his head in place. Diesel moves to the left side and puts his hands on Kenny's jaw, forcing him to open his mouth so Spirit can pour it down his throat. I'm not sure what the fuck is in that cup, but I watch as it flows from the cup and into his mouth. His eyes widen as he struggles not to swallow but once again, they work as a team. Johnny forces his jaw closed as Diesel holds his nose. Spirit rubs up and down on his throat like you would a dog you're trying to get it to swallow a pill. Kenny's eyes roll back in his head and his body jerks as he turns a ghastly greenish color.

Spirit grabs his crotch to get his attention. "Remember what I told you. Do not puke, no matter what. It'll only make it worse for you."

Releasing his junk, she walks to the table, looking at the different tools. I glance at Kenny and I can feel his fear pouring out of him. He catches my eye and the pleading in his shocks me. Before I can say anything, his mouth opens and blood starts to pool out of it. What the fuck did they give him?

"Quinn, please stop this. Walker's the one who made us do that shit to you. If we didn't he would've killed us. Come on, I got kids. Don't do this, please..."

Stone walks over to him and punches him in the face. "Shut the fuck up. Did we tell you you could speak?" Stone punches him again and Kenny's eyes roll before he passes out.

Spirit grabs what looks like bolt cutters. My stomach starts to turn and, as if she knows this, she turns to me with anger in her eyes.

"Don't you dare puke either? I'm not cleaning it up so don't piss me off Quinn."

Shaking, I nod and stand up. I take a moment to 'get my shit together' and move across the room. I lean on the cabinet, my eyes on the cutters in Spirit's hand.

Going to the right side of Kenny, she holds his nose closed until his eyes open up. He glares at her but says nothing. Blood is drooling out of the side of his mouth and his body starts to spasm. His eyes look to the side, trying to see what she's going to do next.

Stone steps up next to her, looking ominous. "Okay, the way this works is we ask a question and you give us an honest answer. If you do this, we won't hurt you. Lie or try to bullshit us, I will let her loose on you and Kenny, believe me, you don't want that. You understand?"

He closes his eyes for a moment then re-opens them, nodding slowly.

Stone takes a step back before he speaks.

"Where is Walker hiding out?" Kenny shakes his head.

"I don't know, honestly. He has a couple of places he can go, but he doesn't tell us where he is, I swear."

As Stone watches him closely, he then glances at Spirit and gives a chin lift. I watch as Spirit takes a syringe and plunges it into Kenny's hand. He lets out a groan, but tries to maintain his composure.

"I don't want you to pass out from the pain, so this is to numb ya just a bit. You'll still feel some pain though," Spirit states with a grin.

After a couple of minutes, I see the team close in on the gurney and Kenny starts to scream. I have no idea why at first, but then I hear it. It's a sound I can't place at first ... crunching? I move so I can see exactly what Spirit's doing, and I'm confused. She has the cutters on Kenny's pinky, but Diesel has another set on, of all things, a chicken leg. As he presses down, the sound I was hearing gets louder. Then, from behind Spirit, Johnny throws a zip lock bag on the tray.

Feeling nauseated, my hand jerks to my mouth as I take a deep breath in through my nose and out through my mouth. As I'm doing this, I also give myself a pep talk. I need to be tough. What in the fuck is in that bag? Shit, it looks like a finger. Between the screaming and the noise of crushing chicken bones, I feel like I'm in the middle of a horror movie.

When the bolt cutters come together on the chicken leg, Diesel lets out a chuckle as Spirit reaches in and pulls the finger out of the baggie opening a small capsule allowing blood to spew all over. To shut Kenny up, Diesel shoves a rag in his mouth as tears pour down his face. His eyes don't leave mine during the whole ordeal.

Stone removes the rag, using it to wipe his face. All it does is put drool and blood on top of his tears. Snot is running out of his nose and the blood is still pooling at the side of his mouth.

"We can make this easy or hard, Kenny. Now, once again, where is he?"

"If I say anything, he'll not only kill me, but my old lady and my kids. Stone, come on. Please don't do this. I swear I'm sorry, don't do this. I'm begging you."

Closing his eyes, Stone once again looks to Spirit who nods. She moves to the tray, picking up the finger, making sure Kenny can see her looking at it. He starts to breathe erratically while she reaches for a long thin tube. When he sees it, he tries to get off the table.

"Fuck no, don't do this. Please don't. I swear I don't know! Damn it, I swear to you I don't know. Holy fuck, Spirit, don't do this to me."

Johnny moves to the middle of the table and I understand what they're planning to do. It's a Foley, the tube that goes in a man's dick so they can pee in a bag. Obviously, that wasn't Spirit's intention. I can actually smell Kenny's fear when Johnny takes the scissors that Diesel offers him and cuts right down the middle of Kenny's boxers. I turn my head when the screams keep getting louder and louder as the man begs for them to stop.

For some sick reason, even though I don't want to watch, I find myself looking between the gaps of my spread fingers. Spirit hasn't even started and Kenny's screeching like a girl. Part of me feels like I should stop it all now, but the other part, the part that was there ten years ago, thinks it's good for the asshole. That really scares me. I'm trying to remove all my emotion.

I watch as Diesel steps up next to Spirit with gloves on and grabs Kenny's limp dick, pulling it to attention. With the tube in her hand, she gets ready to jam it in when I hear Stone yell to her.

"God damn it. Put some lube on that tube, Spirit. I don't want him dead, so make sure he feels it, but don't send him to his grave—not yet, anyway."

Throwing the tube on the bed, she moves back to the tray and brings back a bottle of *KY*. The sounds coming from Kenny are tearing at my soul. How the fuck do they do this and not let it bother them? All the crying, screaming, and begging, is getting under my skin, but when I look at the others, they actually look bored, yet Kenny looks like his eyes are ready to bug out as more snot runs out of his nose. His entire body is taut with what I assume is the pain he's about to be in. I'm watching the tube being lubed by Diesel as Spirit looks on. Something feels off to me. How can she do this shit? I've been through hell and I couldn't even think about completing it, yet she looks like she's at a baseball game, bored out of her mind.

Finally, Diesel passes the Foley to her as he reaches for Kenny's dick again. Johnny steps up and stuffs a clean rag into the Kenny's mouth to shut him up. With my hands covering my eyes, but peeking through just a little, I feel weird. I want so badly for Kenny to feel pain, but I'm honestly feeling guilty about it now that it's all happening.

Trying to figure my shit out, I see Spirit put the end right on the slit of his dick. She looks at him for a minute before she proceeds to shove it in, slow and steady. I can't watch anymore so I turn away, trying to cover my ears so I can't hear the sounds of his agonizing pain.

Not sure what's happening, I turn and walk to the door, then through it and fall to my knees outside. Taking in deep breaths, I try to remain calm, wondering if this was the way to go. After seeing only a little bit of the games and torture, it made me sick. But sitting on my ass on the hard ground, I'm sick enough to not stop it because I know it would only take a word from me to stop it.

Feeling, rather than hearing someone next to me, I look up to see my sister Raven standing here, staring at me. Holy shit, did she see what had just happened? Fuck, I hope not. Remembering Stone's warning about her, I stand and we stare at each other for a moment before she grabs me and wraps me in her arms. I'm not sure if it's because of all the shit that's gone down in the last forty-eight hours, but I stand in my older sister's arms and cry like a baby.

CHAPTER 5

I'm not sure how long we're outside, but eventually I calm down and Raven takes me inside. The twins are already asleep and I don't want to disturb them, but I need to check and make sure they're okay. Walking down the hall after my sister, she first opens one door, where I see Cari fast asleep with her favorite stuffed animal, Tazzy the Purple Elephant, in her arms. Then we move to the room right next to her where I find Benjamin curled up with an action figure in his hand. God, I love and miss my kids, and no matter what, I need to protect them from all the evil shit going on in my life.

Once I'm satisfied, we turn to go back to the kitchen when I hear a gasp and something comes flying towards me. Feeling arms around my waist, I know who it is. My kid sister, Viola, is holding on tight, her head in my neck, rocking us both from side to side. I can't make out what she's saying, but I know that the stress of the last few days has kicked her ass. Viola suffers from depression and doesn't handle change well. She's been on meds for a while now that seem to be working, but they might need to be adjusted. Pulling back, I kiss her cheek and look at her.

"Viola, honey, calm down. Let's take some deep breaths and relax. I'm here and we're all safe. Just try and relax." I feel more than hear her breathing as her body starts to relax and the tautness in her muscles becomes less and less.

Finally she steps back and grabs my hand. 'Thank God you're here, Quinn. I was so frigging worried."

A small laugh escapes at her attempt to be badass. I don't have the heart to tell her frigging isn't a bad word.

"Viola, all is good. Let's go to the kitchen so we can sit and talk. There's a lot I need to share with both you and Raven."

As we head toward the huge kitchen, I see the front door open as Stone, Johnny, and Diesel, enter. I do a quick look to make sure none of Kenny's blood is noticeable on them, but don't see anything. As we meet halfway, we all enter the kitchen with everyone looking for a place to sit. The table is enormous; probably holds ten or twelve, so we all grab a chair. Feeling kind of out of it, I just look around at everyone at the table.   Just as Stone goes to talk, the back door opens and in walks Spirit, her apron covered in fresh blood. Her face has splatters on it, as well as her hair. Both my sisters look at her in horror for a minute, and then Raven starts screaming. Not wanting her to wake the kids, I reach over and grab her by the shoulders and shake her. But when that doesn't work, I crack her in the face, hard.

"Shut the fuck up, Raven. I don't want you to wake up the kids, so please be quiet. I didn't mean to hit you, but you need to be quiet."

I'm not sure if it was me hitting her in the face or the tone in my voice, but she immediately quiets down.

Stone glances at all three of us and I can tell by his expression that he's trying to evaluate the situation between us, and what has started with Kenny in the shed. As he continues to watch my sisters and me, Spirit goes to the fridge, pulls out an apple and crunches down, ripping off a huge section. That this woman can act like nothing out of the ordinary is happening shows me that I probably don't have the guts to do the actual torturing. All these years I've plotted and planned, feeling determined in the knowledge of what I wanted to do to each and every one of those men, I can't even stomach twenty minutes of it, and I was only watching, not participating.

Spirit sits down right next to me and leans back in her chair. "Don't worry, sunshine. He's still breathing ... but barely. Funny thing, though. When questioning him, he told me that if we wanted to know where

Walker was, talk to her." She points at Raven and raises her eyebrows.

Everyone turns to stare at Raven as she starts to tremble under the pressure. No one says anything, but continues to just intimidate her with their stares.

Spirit continues. "From what Kenny says, Raven has been at the Walker's house and places of business quite a bit lately."

At this, I turn towards her in anger.

"What the hell are you playing at, Raven? You've been in contact with that monster since that night? Why? Are you insane? God damn it. If he finds out about my kids, we won't be able to protect them from that sick bastard. Explain to me what he has on you."

Forgetting everyone around me, I rip into my older sister. It's time to get answers, and I want them now.

Stone, Johnny, and Diesel, stand to leave, but thinking they need to know what we're dealing with, I ask them to stay. As they sit back down, Spirit clears her throat and finishes.

"Kenny also told me that somehow, Walker always knows where y'all are; all of you meaning Viola, Raven, and you, Quinn. The family as he calls it in his sick fucking mind. He said he didn't know how, but that at any given time, Walker can find the three of you. That's all I've gotten out of him so far. Figured I'd give him some time to rest and think before I start the next session."

As I glare at my older sister, she puts her head down. "So, Raven, you need to explain this shit right now."

It's so quiet I swear you could hear a pin drop. That is until Raven pushes her chair back and stands awkwardly. Clearing her throat, she looks around the table slowly, including the men in her glance till she finally lands on me. Tears are running down her face as she tries to compose herself.

"I never wanted you to know, Quinn. You've been through so much and I didn't want to add to your stress, but it's time to let it out. I need to move forward and so do the rest of us. Walker has controlled my life for way too long. Just so you both know, Quinn and Viola, I never gave anything to him that was worthwhile."

Running her hands through her hair, then up and down her face, I watch her try to even out her breathing. Not sure why, I grab her hand at the same time Viola grabs her other hand.

"Before Walker's evil was revealed and Mom and Dad shipped him to the counselor, there were times when he would come into my room, just to hang out, or that was what he said. At first I thought he was lonely and just needed someone in the family on his side. I tried, really I did, to understand what he would tell me, but frankly, it scared the shit out of me. Sometimes he would bring in the carcasses of the dead animals he tortured and killed to show me, like he was bringing me a gift or something. I hated those 'things' in my bedroom, but was becoming more and more fearful of him and his temper. The night that his true colors were revealed was when he brought the cat in he tortured? He had the body in a garbage bag so I really didn't see what he did until to my utter horror; he pulled out a baby kitten, still in the birth sack. I screamed and screamed until he threw the bag down and came at me, cracking me in the face. At that moment, it finally dawned on me that Walker was sick. Not only was he sick, but also psychotic. He found joy in killing a pregnant cat.

When I was able to control my emotions and my tears had slowed to sniffles, I tried to get out of my room, but he had other ideas. Remember I was still a kid, seventeen years old and innocent. When my 'brother' approached me with a look in his eyes, it froze me on the spot. His eyes got this crazy look in them as they roamed over my body. My mind was going crazy and I made an attempt to escape, trying to run to the door, but he caught me by the shoulders, pulling me back against him. It was then I knew his intentions as he ground his hips into my butt. I felt *it*. He turned me and threw me on the bed as he pulled his shirt over his head. I was so stunned; I never even tried to get away. I lay there on my childhood bed as he violently raped me with his hands wound tight around my neck. When he was done, he dressed and from his back pocket, he pulled out a switchblade. Pushing my bloody thighs apart, his hands held down my thigh as he carved something into it. He motioned for me to remain quiet and still. In my shock, I did as I was told."

Moving away from the table, she raises her skirt to reveal what was done to her years ago. My hand goes to my mouth as Viola's loud gasp is heard by each of us. On Raven's upper thigh, there's a "W" with the number 2 next to it. Oh my God, my poor sister. I quickly stand and reach for her, pulling her close to me as Viola comes up and hugs both of us. We start to cry together as we slide to the ground, our arms still holding onto each other.

CHAPTER 6

After what feels like hours, I'm finally able to get both my sisters calm enough to get some sleep after Raven bared her battered soul of all that is Walker. He is a heartless son of a bitch. If he were in front of me, I wouldn't think twice about torturing and killing him. He ruined our family, one person at a time.

Heading to the kitchen to get something to drink, I walk into Stone and his crew, still sitting at the table in the midst of a pretty heated conversation from the looks on their faces. All heads turn my way as I tentatively step to the fridge.

"I'm just getting something to drink. I'll be out of your way in a minute."

Stone is watching me closely. I can feel his heated gaze on my body. As I turn to leave, I hear someone clear his or her throat. Expecting it to be Stone, I turn to see Diesel holding out a chair next to him.

"Come on, Quinn. Sit down here for a minute. We need to figure out what we're going to do with the information Raven shared tonight."

At the mention of my sister's name, Diesel's face looks pained. I don't even want to think about what that could mean. I take the seat and look around the table, finally stopping on Spirit's face.

"Spirit, I need you to help me. I'm not sure that I can do what you do, but there has to be something that I can handle. They need to pay for what they've done to my family, each and every last one of those fuckers."

"Honey, don't wanna add to your distress, but you don't have it in you, not at all. You have a heart and that will always hold you back."

"Come on. I know that it appears as if I can't handle what you were doing to Kenny, but that was before the information Raven just shared. Please, I need to do this so my family can move on, safely."

Everyone sits quietly for a minute, looking at each other. Somehow they seem to communicate without words. Stone nods. They all get up and leave the room, leaving us to stare at each other.

"Quinn, I know Raven's reveal has you pissed right now, I get that, but Spirit's right. You can't handle the torture part of this, no matter what you think. Even the mind fuck we pulled on Kenny freaked you out. Spirit's one of the best at mind fucking prisoners into thinking that they're being tortured when in fact, they're not. Even with the job we do, we aren't monsters. We were discussing this when you came in. We think we have a plan, but I need your input. Instead of killing them all, how about we follow your later journals and financially and emotionally ruin them—bring them to their knees. Then they can be turned over to spend the rest of their days on earth in an eight by eight cell, rotting by themselves, alone. What do you think? Would that give you the vengeance you seek?"

"What does that even mean? How can I ruin them? Do they even have anything to take? And what would I do with their money, because I sure don't want it? Help me understand."

Stone gets up and grabs a beer out of the fridge, then sits next to me. He grabs my hand and glides his thumb across the top of mine, which begins to calm me.

"This is what we're talking about. Each man has huge amounts of wealth from their criminal involvement with Walker, both financial and material wealth. Some have multiple homes, cars, antiques, anything and everything you can imagine. So, Johnny came up with the idea of getting all the info we can on them; talk to their families, see if they are in fact good husbands and fathers. Depending on what we gather, that will help in our decisions for our next steps. If they are decent to their family members, you decide how far we take it. Personally, I doubt they even know the definition of family, but we'll find out. If not, we'll destroy them, help the families relocate and start fresh, and make sure they're financially secure. After we've done that, each man will be turned into the FBI and prosecuted to the fullest extent of the law. Would that help you heal Quinn? Finally put your past to rest without all the torture and bloodshed? Don't get me wrong, Spirit will still do her thing, but you won't be involved and you'll know nothing about what's been done. Can you move forward and put the demons back in hell where they belong?"

Closing my eyes, I feel his hand caress my cheek ever so softly. Inside me a war is raging. This man is making me nuts. If I go by the past and his actions, then I don't want anything to do with him. But if looking at the present and all he's done for me, then I think it's something I want to explore.

Leaning away from his hand, I open my eyes. "Stone, I'm going to be honest. The last few days have fucked with my head. I thought I knew what I wanted and how my revenge would go if the chance ever presented itself. Then you walk into my life, or should I say back into my life. You alone are enough to fucking drive me crazy, but then your crew, who have dedicated years to protect us, adds to the fucking situation. Not to mention that crazy fuck Walker and his mess of assholes. At this moment I have no idea what to do or how to proceed, but I do need a favor. Can I have five minutes with Kenny? I need to ask him a couple of questions."

Her beautiful eyes tug at my heart. Knowing I can't say no to her, I counter her request.

"Okay. I'll give you five minutes with him, but not alone. You can pick who stays with you, but to get this, I want your word that after you visit him, we come back in here and have a serious conversation. There's so much you need to hear and I want it to be from me. Deal?

CHAPTER 7

After coming to an agreement, both Quinn and I walk out to the shed. The lack of noise is probably not a good thing, but I slowly open the door and Quinn walks in before me. As soon as we enter and Quinn takes a breath, she turns to me and whispers. "What the hell is that horrible smell? I don't remember smelling it earlier." Damn, Spirit. I told her no more tonight.

"Stay the fuck here. Let me check it out." Moving around her, I go to the room that Kenny's being held in. I already know what the smell is, it's burning flesh.

Fucking Spirit.

It's one of her favorite things to do to them to shut them up. As I enter the room, my eyes immediately move to Kenny's feet, which are blackened. His eyes are glazed and drool is running down his chin while Spirit sits at the desk, playing solitaire on her laptop.

Trying to keep my voice down, I whisper roughly, "What the fuck, Spirit? I thought we all agreed to let Quinn call this one? This was not part of the plan, so explain this to me ... *now*."

"He was being a dick, even after I warned him, so I shut him up. It was either burn his feet or cut his tongue out. Did I make the wrong choice Stone?"

The twinkle in her eyes tells me she's trying to pull my chain. Before I can even reply, I hear the gasp behind me and swear under my breath. Doesn't anyone listen to me anymore?

"Holy shit. What happened to his feet?"

Approaching her, I try to keep my temper controlled but it's late, I'm tired, and this woman just pulls all my strings.

"Did I not make myself clear? I told you to stay back by the door until I cleared it. Don't you understand fuckin' English? What do I have to do for you to listen to me, spank your ass like the child you are acting like? Is that what you want?"

Her sharp intake of breath is my only warning before she comes at me, hands fisted. The first punch hits me straight on the chin, which takes my breath away. The second hit is to the balls.

"Don't you ever fucking talk to me like that. I'm not your whore, girlfriend, or fuck buddy. I do what I want, when I want, never forget that. Understand, asshole?"

Trying to breathe through the pain as I grab my balls, nothing comes out. I'm in shock, until I hear Spirit laugh. She's laughing at me for getting my ass kicked by Quinn. I'll never live this one down.

"Fuck, Quinn, why'd you do that? I don't want to expose you to shit that's gonna upset you so yeah, I was being bossy, but I had your best interest at heart and this is how you pay me back? What the fuck?" Turning, I walk past Quinn to the door, slamming it open and walking out.

I watch him leave, then turn to Spirit. "Is he always so sensitive? Shit, I didn't even hit his balls that hard." Spirit looks at me for a minute then busts out laughing so hard that she's bending over, holding her stomach.

"Girl, this is gonna be fun. I haven't seen someone under his skin, like, ever. I can't wait to see the next round between you two, bruiser."

Losing myself in the moment, I totally forget we have Kenny secured to the bed. Hearing him moaning cruelly brings me back to the here and now. I can see that Spirit really fucked his feet up. What the hell are we doing?

"Can you take that off his mouth? I want to talk to him."

Spirit walks over and removes the rag and tape from his mouth. I'm actually shocked when she grabs a water bottle and gently pours some into Kenny's mouth, even lifting his head so he doesn't choke. When she finishes, she steps back, but doesn't go far.

"Kenny, I need to ask you some questions and I'm hoping you'll give me some truthful answers. What you give me here will determine the outcome of what will happen to you, okay?"

He looks away from me to Spirit. His gaze is longer and more intense, making me feel like I'm intruding on something, but can't put my finger on it. Before I can ask what that was about, Spirit lets out what sounds like a growl.

"Answer her, you stupid asshole. Don't make me force you. You know I'll do it without thinking twice, Kenny."

He watches her for a moment longer before he shifts his gaze back to me. The pain I see in his eyes is startling. He quickly recovers as he blinks, adjusting his face to a bored; 'don't give a fuck' look.

"Whatever, Quinn. Let's get this over with. You've been waiting for years for this opportunity so let's see if you truly have the stomach for what you want to do. Have you ever killed anything? Tortured a living being? It changes everything in your life, especially you as a human being, so good luck living with your choices. They'll be your downfall someday and you won't even know who you are anymore."

He turns his head to look at the opposite side of the room. I'm confused at what he's just said to me as I had no idea he felt any type of remorse for any of his prior actions, but that's what I'm here to find out.

"All I want is some closure, Kenny, that's it. So, my first question is how were you able to do what you did to me and live with that? What type of person are you?

Watching him closely, I swear he smirks before he hides behind a look that makes it appear that he's sorry.

"Quinn, you have to believe me that it was all Walker. He would've killed anyone who wasn't on board. That wasn't me. I'm not a violent person, I swear to God."

I hear Spirit's snarky remark, 'Whatever, asshole,' but I don't turn around because I'm watching Kenny, closely, and he can't hide the look he shoots her. His face is full of anger and contempt. He doesn't realize I've been waiting to see the real him. Stone coached me to be prepared for anything, and he was right again.

As I'm about to call Kenny on his bullshit, we hear a door open and slam shut. Waiting to see whose approaching, Spirit and I wait patiently while Kenny waits impatiently.

Johnny, Diesel, and Stone's faces all look angry, but there's something else there too that I can't read as I don't know them well enough yet. Diesel clears my confusion and lack of knowledge quickly.

"So Kenny, you're a family man, right? A devoted husband and father, that's what ya told us earlier. How many kids you got?"

Kenny gulps loudly and his eyes shift left to right. "Um, well, I have three kids," he replies as his eyes look everywhere, but not at Diesel.

"So you only have three kids Kenny? You sure? Is that your final answer?"

I hear snorts and laughter from the other guys but Diesel only glares at Kenny, waiting for his answer.

"Well, no, I ... well, I had ... shit. This is really hard. We lost a kid a couple of years ago in a bad accident."

Suddenly the room temperature feels as if we're in an icebox. Before I can even register what's happening, I hear Kenny scream, followed by begging. Diesel has his hands around the man's throat, choking the life out of him. Both Stone and Johnny are trying to remove his hands from Kenny's throat, but to no avail. I rush to the other side of the gurney, grabbing Diesel's hands.

"Diesel, what are you doing? Stop this right now, you asshole. I don't want him killed. We need to talk to him and find out about Walker. Please, Diesel, let him go."

Diesel's eyes are pained. Struggling to hold it together, he finally takes a deep breath and releases Kenny. "Quinn, you have no idea what this asshole did to his own kid—his beautiful, innocent child—because he was drunk and high on drugs. Go ahead, dickhead. Tell her what ya did, and don't try to make it sound like an accident because the only reason your ass isn't in jail is because of Walker and his connections."

I turn from Diesel to Kenny. I have no idea what I'm about to hear, but I know deep down it's not going to be good.

Fuck me. What the hell made me think being anywhere near any of these assholes was a good idea?

CHAPTER 8

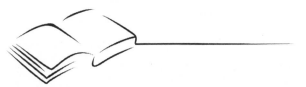

Kenny glares at me and actually spits in my direction. "You think you're all that, don't you, Quinn. Remember, I know different, bitch. Been there, in your cunt, in your ass, and in your mouth. You ain't any different than any other bitch I've fucked."

His words shock me. I slap him in the face, not once, not twice, but I don't stop smacking him until Stone pulls me into him, his arms wrapping under my breasts and holding me back while whispering in my ear. "Sugar, he's trying to make you forget about Diesel's question. Think before you proceed, Quinn. Kenny's is playing you, even though he's restrained. Take a minute to get your head where it needs to be. *You* are the one in control, not him."

Stone continues to hold me close, but I never take my eyes from Kenny's. His fixed look never wavers and the smirk on his face tells me that he's done playing games. He knows his gig was up, so why fake it now?

Finally in control of myself, I demand an answer to Diesel's question. "Kenny, what happened to your child? They'll tell me anyway so just spit it out. What the fuck did you do?"

By the end of my question, I'm screaming, losing my shit. The only thing I can hear in the room is my uneven breathing as Kenny and I have a stare down. This asshole isn't going to give me anything. I can recognize the defiance in his eyes. He's shutting me down, so I look to Diesel. "Tell me what happened to the child, Diesel, please?"

Diesel grabs a tablet from Spirit's desk and walks to where Stone and I are standing. He clicks the screen a few times and once he's satisfied, he gets closer and reveals what he knows.

"About two to three years ago, this ass wipe," he points to Kenny, "was married with four kids. It wasn't bliss, but they seemed to be happy, or that was what they portrayed to the outside world. No one knew the hell that was going on inside that house. Kenny shared his 'wife' with the entire crew, from the top being Walker to the guy on the bottom, Jazz Man. His wife, Joann, had enough and left with the children. She went to a shelter for help and they provided it. They put her somewhere that even Walker couldn't penetrate. That was until the day Jazz Man saw Kenny's son, Georgie, coming out of a store. He grabbed the kid and took him back to their compound. These motherfuckers spent hours torturing this poor eleven-year-old child, trying to find out where Joann was. They were worried she had been around too much and would be able to sell them out. Finally, Kenny had enough and put a bullet in his son's head, right between his eyes. *No father ... no man* would ever do such a thing to a child. Only a heartless fucking coward would do such a thing, and that's exactly what Kenny here is, a worthless, piece of shit, coward."

It takes me a couple of minutes before I can absorb what Diesel has just told me. Yeah, they fucked me up, but I was an adult. But to do that to a helpless child is unacceptable. The anger ... no, it's more than anger. It's unexplainable, but the fury I feel makes my blood boil. I had no control back in that loft years ago, but to have a child who didn't stand a chance, couldn't even fight those men to save his own life disgusts me on a level I can't even comprehend. Finding this out and realizing that these assholes had no regard for life, even a child's, makes this moment so much more than my pain. I feel so emotional knowing that poor young Georgie's life ended way too soon. The need to make Kenny suffer overtakes me.

Feeling Stone's arms relax around me, I take a step away from him. His arms fall away and I walk around to Spirit's table, which holds her tools and pick the one tool with a handle.

I approach the gurney, arm raised, ready to let the hatchet fall when I'm grabbed from behind. The hatchet's snatched from my hand and I scream in anger. Time seems to stand still as I watch the blade first hit Kenny's chest, then cut immediately through as he screams bloody murder. I feel absolutely nothing at all. I don't even see who did the deed. All I can see is an unknown child with a bullet in his head, put there by his father.

With the hatchet embedded in Kenny's chest, I watch him take in his last breaths. He's dead, and it's all because of me.

CHAPTER 9

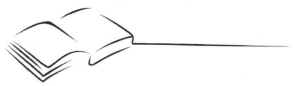

Stone's hands run slowly up and down my back, massaging away the tightness. As my mind begins to clear and the thoughts of what happened in the shed causes me to hyperventilate.

"Quinn, calm the fuck down. Breathe in through your nose and out through your mouth. Come on sugar; take it easy you're safe. Damn it. Johnny, get a brown bag for Quinn."

I hear running, and then a brown bag is being shoved in my face. I take it and breathe in and out, getting myself back to normal.

"Thanks, Johnny. I'll call if we need ya. Wait, can you do me a favor first and check on Quinn's kids?" Johnny nods and leaves.

"What happened, Stone ... what did I do? If someone hadn't have grabbed that hatchet I would have killed him. I was ready to fucking kill him with a hatchet. Oh my God, what have I done?"

Stone comes around and squats in front of me, gently grasping my face in his hands. "Sugar, not gonna lie to you, and I never will. Yeah, Kenny's dead, but I don't want you freakin' out or losin' it. He deserved so much more than what he got, and I get why you lost it. However, I need you to hold it together because this is just the beginning of your road to revenge. This one was actually easy. I know, wrong choice of words, but you get what I mean. We need to have that talk right now because there's still a chance, slim as it is, to turn back and forget about getting revenge. The situation is getting hot now so if we go the distance, we won't be able to stop till it's done, you understand?"

Looking into those green eyes, I actually feel a calm come over me. It starts in my head and travels down my body. My breathing slows, as my heart rate gets back to normal. Even the tension in my muscles starts to relax. Something about Stone, and fuck if I can figure it out, seems to really bring me back to my center. Even though certain parts of me, deep down hate him, I can't deny his effect on me any longer. There are parts of me that want to get to know him so much more.

"Why are you doing this Stone? I mean really, who does this shit for someone they don't even know? You have to make me understand because I'm freaking the fuck out and need to know why you and those people out there want to help my family and me."

Taking a moment to get my thoughts together, I finally realize the time has come to give her what she wants.

"Quinn, in one way or another, Walker and his father are responsible for chaos in our families. Over the years they've trampled on many lives, but we all found each other because of our own desire for revenge. Can you start to see why we've had your back all these years? *You* are the missing piece, what we need for us to get *our* revenge. I'm not gonna break confidences and tell ya how each person in my crew has been affected by Walker, but trust me when I say that every one of us know where you're coming from."

She nods, so I continue.

"Now is the time for you to decide what our next move is. Once Kenny doesn't report in to Walker, shit is gonna hit the fan. So, if you wanna back off and just move on with your life, that's fine, but we will need to get something in place for you and your family. Otherwise, we need to put our cards on the table, holding nothing back. I know you're thinking I know everything about you, but there are still things you're hiding, right? Wait don't answer just yet. Let me start so you get where I'm coming from."

Grabbing my hand, he pulls me up from what appears to be a futon and we walk to an area that has a table and chairs. I sit as Stone asks, "Do you want something to drink, sugar?"

"Water is fine, thanks."

As he grabs two waters, I look around; average room, no personal items. Water comes into view and I grab it as he sits next to me.

"Okay. I'm not sure where to start, but here it goes." Stone begins to tell me his story.

CHAPTER 10

I run my hands through my hair nervously as I try to control the overwhelming feeling of the room closing in on me. I watch Quinn stare at me, knowing she's waiting impatiently for me to begin. I have never told anyone, not even Johnny or Diesel, what I'm about to tell Quinn. Can I finally put myself out there, open the wounds, and let the poison out? Fuck, I want to, but it's been so long and to be honest, I'm scared. Yeah, the badass Stone is afraid to tell a woman about his past. I shake my head as my hand massages the tight muscles in my neck. It's time I pull my own head out of the sand.

"You know that Walker and I were 'friends' back in the day. I had no idea how damaged and ill he actually was until the

102

night they killed your parents and raped you. Shit, let me back up. Growing up, we did a lot of crazy fucking shit. As little boys, we would go down to the pond to capture frogs to torture and kill."

She's observing me with a strange look in her eyes, but I can't stop now, so I continue forward.

"As we got older, my parents started to get worried and wanted me to break off my friendship with Walker. By that time we were in what, middle school? My parents forbid me from hanging with him. Being a know-it-all I didn't listen and snuck around, still hanging with Walker and his boys. I can't believe you and I never met. Believe me, we all knew about the three sisters Walker was obsessed with. I think I fell in love with you by freshman year, just from hearing his descriptions of you, Quinn."

At my admission, I refuse to look at her. "Feeling those feelings, I knew in my heart that Walker would never let me or anyone of us near any of you. As we grew older, it became apparent that he had a sick obsession with you and your sisters. He spoke about your parents rarely, but you three he talked about all the fuckin' time, and that's not an exaggeration. A couple months before the counselor incident, he went on a rampage one night. We were hanging out at my house in the basement. I can't remember why, but Walker was anxious; seemed like his mind was elsewhere and no matter what any of us did, he was getting pissed more and more as the night wore on. Donnie said something about what was going on at home and Walker grabbed him by the throat, throwing him against the wall. Donnie was turning blue and as I watched Walker, I saw for the first time who the real Walker was. He had this sick smile and gleam in his eyes. He was actually enjoying the pain he was inflicting on Donnie as he watched his lips turning blue. It took all of us to pull Walker off before he killed him. Needless to say, that was when I saw up close and personal that my childhood friend was a raving lunatic. From that point on, I started pulling away from that crowd, tried to buckle down in school and really listen to what my parent's wanted from me. Time went by and after he beat up the counselor and ended up in that facility, I lost all contact. It really sucked cause I had no excuse then to keep you in my sight.

"With all of this and time moving on I kind of lost track of Walker until the night of your rape. I didn't have a clue how sick he truly was. My view from the window was like watching a horror flick. Quinn, I have no words to explain how I felt that night. I'd already started my training for the government after the academy and heard through the ranks that Walker was on their radar, and I didn't realize how far his dad's reach was. It went all the way up the ladder. Even after he died, Walker just stepped in his shoes, so to speak.

After they killed your parent's, then Raven and Viola escaped, I was kind of in shock. I watched a childhood friend commit murder not once, but twice. Then they all surrounded you and my God, Quinn, I couldn't do anything. I can't imagine how you felt, but I was scared shitless for the first time in my life; fucking scared out of my mind. Then it began and I just stood there after calling my captain. That call should have brought in the cavalry, but instead I got nothin'. I watched those animals rape you repeatedly as I stood outside a window doing absolutely nothing. Every time I tried to move my feet, they seemed glued to the ground. I felt the tears first running down my face when Walker sodomized you first, then gave you to his crew. I had nothing to give you but me, Quinn; I didn't want to walk away and leave you alone so I got your attention and gave you me. I tried to let you know you weren't alone.

"When I finally accepted and realized that there would be no help coming, I put in a 911 call, but by then your sisters had made it to the police station and they were on their way. By the time I got through all the necessary paperwork and de-briefing, you were in the hospital, sedated. I spent the next twenty-seven hours with you in the hospital and only left when your sisters came to see you, but they were both in shock themselves.

"After you spoke to the police, gave your statement and were released, my opportunity to speak to you was taken away. You and your sisters seemed to have disappeared so I tried to concentrate on busting Walker. But something, or someone, was holding up the investigation and when I looked into it, I found out my captain was the one. I brought that motherfucker down. Because of his greed, you lost your parents and something more ... a part of you was lost that night, Quinn. I know, because I lost a part of me too. The guilt has been eating me alive since then. That's why when this task force was formed, I signed up immediately, even before we were told that a detail would be your shadow."

Standing up, I stretch as my body feels like it's been stuffed into a box and needs some release. Taking a quick glance at

Quinn, I see she looks like she's deep in her own head. Her face is looking past me, eyes glazed and dilated. Not sure what's going on with her, I reach down and run my hand down her cheek. Her wet eyes shoot to me as I realize that she's reliving that horrific night. Immediately, the familiar feeling of protecting Quinn rises in my chest.

"Sugar, come on. I didn't mean to bring you back there. Look at me, I'm right here and you're safe, I promise."

"I'm good, Stone, really. You're right. It took me back for a minute, but I'm good, so go on, please."

Sitting next to her, I lean back in the chair, hands across my chest.

"When I realized that my detail, some of them people you've met, were given the orders to keep you and your sisters under surveillance, I knew that was my chance to not make up to you what happened, but to keep you safe. I took it seriously. By that time, Johnny, Diesel, and Spirit had gotten really tight. Johnny and I had gone through some shit together so he knew where I was coming from."

"What do you mean, you and Johnny went through some serious shit?"

"After all the shit went down with you, I kind of lost it. Especially after my captain was caught and put away for the fucking loser he turned out to be. I lost faith in everyone, including myself. Started to fall into the darkness as my guilt over everything that had happened took over. I worked with Johnny on a ransom case we both were involved in. The case was different than yours, but some of the stuff that happened reminded me of all the shit you went through. I went into my head, but Johnny being Johnny, pulled me out of it. He taught me how to deal with what I was putting myself through. Damn, those were the days, Quinn. We were such a badass team. Between working and living together, we partied together. There was nothing we couldn't do. Shit, the women that threw themselves at us ... shit, sorry. But you get where I'm going."

Hearing a small giggle, I see Quinn barely holding on. As I watch, she loses her shit and lets it out, holding her sides as she laughs out loud.

"Thanks for that, Stone. I needed a laugh. You act like I can't put two and two together, to come up with two players?"

"Well, I owe Johnny my life. I was dipping into the darker aspects of life and don't bother asking, Quinn. I'm not going there. Just know that my guilt was eating away at me. The first time Johnny asked me to go with him to the tattoo parlor, I was like 'whatever', but on the way, he explained that he had a case go really bad and needed to let it go. I asked him what he was talking about and he told me that whenever he needed to let go of the pain or darkness, he would get a tattoo or a piercing. Now at this time, I didn't realize the work he had done already. So long story short, that's the night I got my first tat. It's the one line tattoo right on my rib cage in black scroll; the words *'Bear No Malice'*. Didn't want to put anything with the word forgive so I used these words for a reminder to myself, so every time it became a burden, I would see this phrase and it brought everything into perspective. Over the years, I used my art and piercings as a way to deal with my life's hardest struggles."

"So what happened that made you pierce your cock Stone?"

Looking her in the eye, I give it to her straight.

"You, Quinn ... you happened. It was the first time you slept with that guy you picked up from the bar. I couldn't handle it and got drunk on Tequila with Johnny and went to see our guy. Told him I needed what hurt the most and he smiled a wicked grin, then he pierced my dick."

CHAPTER 11

Holy shit! Did Stone just say he pierced his dick because I slept with some guy ... a one-night stand at that? What the fuck? Who does that, and why? Struggling with all he's shared, and even knowing all this, I still have that part of me that's so mad at him for that night. I know that in all reality, he couldn't have done anything, but it doesn't change that tiny part of me that can't help but blame him.

"So you're telling me that because of me, you pierced and inked your body?" Not waiting for an answer, I continue. "Stone, listen closely to me. I hear what you're telling me and know that I truly appreciate all that has been done for my family and me. Sincerely, all of you have my gratitude, especially for what you're doing for my children. Now, with that said, I don't know if I can ever truly forgive you one hundred percent. That night broke me—tore me apart and killed a part of me I can never get back. I want to be as honest as you have been with me. There's a part of me that's infatuated with you. I mean shit, look at you—the bad boy every woman dreams about. Fucking hot ass body, gorgeous face, and those Goddamn green eyes that look at a woman like you're starving to make her yours. I'm so damn confused, Stone, and what happened the other night didn't help. Well, it did, but didn't, if you know what I mean."

He smiles that devilish grin, but says nothing.

"What happened tonight made me realize that I don't have it in me to kill someone. Even if someone hadn't grabbed the hatchet, I'm not sure I could have finished him off. How can you act like it's no big deal killing someone?" Hearing the shaking in my voice, I take a deep breath.

"However, I don't want the last three men and Walker to get off scot free. What are our options? Can we come up with something that will hurt them but not kill them? Or if death is the answer, I don't know if I can even ask or assume that one of you will do that for me. That's asking for something no one has the right to ask of another human being. Not sure what this means, but know that I do appreciate everything that has been done. But my main objective is those two kids in the other room. I need to be their mom from now on and a sister to Raven and Viola. I can't live in my head or those books you brought with us here. Those are tools to help me heal, nothing more. I can't dwell on how revenge has fed my soul for so long. Looking at it now, I'm not sure if the journals were helpful, or a way to keep me from going insane. I could never be that person who can do the stuff Spirit does and live with myself. How she does it, I don't know, but I can't."

Stone watches for a second or two without saying a word, then he lays it on me.

"Let's take a minute and think about this. You realize now that you can't kill them.

Well, just to fill you in on a little secret, we all knew this already. Just because you can write it down, doesn't mean you can carry it out in the real world. There are options, and we need to work out the best way to move forward. You can just let it go and move on with your life, or we can hurt them in other ways. Each one of them has secrets that we can use against them; break them financially and emotionally. We'll take everything away from them till they have nothing. Then we can go in and bring them to their knees, and finally have them arrested. With the evidence we've already accrued over the years, they'll never see the light of day. Diesel's been working his magic with obtaining information, or I should say secrets that most people wouldn't want revealed. Each of these three guys are into some sick fucking shit, and we haven't even gotten into Walker. So we have four men who need to be taught a lesson, a lesson that will last a lifetime. Hopefully, in the long run, this will all help to protect other women and children.

"So, can you handle this? Will you be able to live with yourself when we're through and these men are either incarcerated or dead? I don't expect an answer tonight, but I want you to take some time and really think about it. Time is ticking and whatever you decide, we need to make sure all are on board. There's a lot we need to get lined up before we can start taking these sick motherfuckers down. I'll give you tonight to think on it."

She doesn't hesitate at giving me a single nod before she stands and leaves the room without a word. I watch until I don't see her any longer and I wait for her decision.

CHAPTER 12

Sitting in my room after spending some time playing two different board games with my children, Cari and Benjamin, reflecting on how very lucky I am to have these two great kids. We played one of their board games and watching their personalities and their interaction with each other makes my heart happy. God I love those kids.

Thinking about my conversation with Stone, I rock back and forth on my bed. Going through everything that Stone revealed to me fills my head. Not sure what to do or how to move past this night, I grab a couple of my blue journals, the revenge books I've written in for years. God, what the hell was I thinking, writing down all my thoughts in anger? The shit I wanted to do to those men who took everything from me is written in my hand. First my mom, then my dad and finally my innocence—for myself. They took from me my sexuality. Yes my sexuality. Since that night, I've only taken and never could find a way to work towards a relationship with anyone, including the closeness of a sexual relationship. No, not me. I stayed closed up and had one-night stands only. I tried once to have a relationship, but I kept up my wall, not letting him touch me, the *real* me. Had counselors that tried to help only made things worse by encouraging me to write down my hate. It only fed the fire.

Reading journal after journal, my eyes start to burn, but I can't put them down. I feel like I'm seeing myself for the first time, what I went through and how I dealt with it, and how I'm still trying to deal with it. All these years have been me trying to find myself and get back some of what those animals took from me.

Between Stone's revealing conversation and all my blue journals, I'm feeling something I haven't felt in over ten years:

peace, forgiveness, and acceptance. I feel like I'm finally ready to move forward for my kids, for Raven and Viola and myself as we have given up so much. Poor Raven, who has been living in her own hell for years.

With Kenny gone, the only ones left are Dirk, Jazz Man (Jimbo), Marco, and Walker, and knowing the world today, I go to social media to start my search for the rest.

Grabbing my tablet, I start to do my own research. Probably not as in-depth as Diesel's, but he doesn't know what I'm looking for. Women can find out shit men never think to look for.

I start with Dirk. It takes a bit, but I find him on Facebook. He's never been married, and no mention of kids. He doesn't mention any type of occupation and I know why. He works for Walker, which is all illegal shit. The main thing Dirk posts about is how he's a baseball coach for young boys. At first I'm surprised because it doesn't seem like something this pervert would be into. Didn't think he had the patience or heart to work with children.

Remembering the night of the rape, he was brutal when he took his turn. Besides raping me, he got off on hitting and biting me. It got so bad that Walker had to pull him off me at one point, saying something about keeping me in one piece. Thinking on it now, it seems like a strange thing to say.

Going to Google, I do a search and I'm surprised to see that over the last ten years, there have been four young boys from baseball, soccer, football, and hockey teams gone missing. One was found dead a year and half after he disappeared, tortured beyond anything the cops said they had ever seen before. The other three were still missing. Dirk was a coach on the same exact teams at the same time the kids went missing. I have an awful feeling as I mark down dates and the kids' names. Holy fuck, he's a pedophile. If this is true, he deserves to die in a painful fucking way.

Next is Jazz Man, or Jimbo. From our conversation earlier, he was the one that found Kenny's boy and grabbed him for Kenny so once again I search social media. This asshole has been married and divorced three times, has four kids with three different women, and just got married to wife number four. She's a much younger woman and from the pics posted, she's knocked up. Well, isn't that just great.

He works at a bank in the city and he's been there for a while. Nothing is popping out at me or setting off alarms, so I write down all the information about his marriages, kids, work, and new pregnant wife. I'll see if Diesel can find something.

Marco is last. Now this guy confused the hell out of me that night. He was scared, didn't want to be involved. He even offered to keep guard outside. When Raven and Viola got away, Marco wanted to go after them. Walker didn't let him and sent another one of his guys. When it was Marco's turn at me, he begged Walker not to make him. Walker beat the fuck out of him before he told him to pull his shit together and get busy. Marco tried to be gentle and not hurt me. Remembering this after all these years, I realize I assumed every one of them was cruel, but Marco wasn't. I check on him anyway and find that he's married, has been for almost eight years with two children. Marco works at a factory while his wife is a nurse's aide at the hospital they took me to after the rape. Nothing looks out of place, but I write down everything I can find, just to be sure.

Walker. Walker doesn't have any social media accounts. I have no information about him, but I'm positive that Stone and the guys do. I'll have to wait to get that in the morning, or at least in a few hours as I glance at the clock to see it's already after three in the morning. Fuck, what am I doing? I have no idea, but after Stone left the decision up to me, I knew I had to make sure that we were doing the right thing. Maybe not right, but I'm not assuming that these guys didn't make a mistake and then change their lives for the better, but I'd rather know for sure before making an uninformed decision about someone's life.

Next I spread my notes across the bed, trying to find a common interest or something besides Walker that keeps them together. Looking at my tablet and phone, I notice some of the pictures they have posted are about parties, kid's birthdays, and all of them are always together. So, besides their criminal activities, they still all associate with one another. Walker is keeping them tight, not letting in strangers so he can control their every move. He may be a psychopath, but he's also a genius. He's kept the most loyal at his side, and others from that night have disappeared over the years. From what Stone and Johnny stated earlier is that Walker removed them; the weakest links of the group.

After working on this for hours, I gather the notes and place them on the nightstand, along with my blue journals. These are the most recent that Stone brought along. Looking at the books, I realize that these books were my only way to survive over these last ten years. All my memories, thoughts, and fears are written in each and every book. I feel a sense of relief as I realize for the first time ever that I'm going to be all right. Maybe not tonight, but eventually I'll have control of my life and move forward with my future, whatever that may be. No more Walker, or any of those assholes, not even the memories of that night—just my kids, my sisters, and me.

Turning the light off, I get comfortable in this strange bed. I've come to the conclusion that Stone, like me, was a victim of Walker's. Worse for Stone, he thought they were friends, but my cousin didn't know how to be a friend. It was all about what he could get from someone or how he could use him or her. Stone got caught up in Walker's sick shit and it fucked him up. Then he saw the extent that Walker's madness took him to, along with the betrayal of his own Captain. It's cut him deeply.

Finding Johnny, Diesel, and Spirit was his saving grace. I smile to myself, thinking he pierced his dick because I fucked someone I couldn't even remember.

Sitting up, I grab my tablet and look up male genital piercings, just out of curiosity. After reading for about ten minutes, I put the tablet down and settle back in.

Stone Myanto isn't a monster, not even close. He was a man, who for whatever reason, cared enough about me that for the last ten years, he and his friends have protected my kids, my sisters, and myself with no gain to them whatsoever.

As I start to drift off, I see Stone, when he was sitting on the side of my bed, naked. When I looked down his carved body and saw his huge cock and the piercings, knowing now why he got them, makes my body shiver in excitement. This is my last thought as sleep pulls me under and my mind finally shuts off.

CHAPTER 13

The last two weeks have been crazy. Between having Stone so close and wanting to have him, along with the decision I made late that night in bed, it's started the beginning of the end.

When I told Stone my decision, he looked at me for a long time before pulling me close to give me a gentle kiss and a tight hug. After that, he gathered the troops and we started to plan ... and plan ... and plan some more. Poor Diesel hasn't left the area full of computers for more than a couple breaks here and there. The mad talent that Diesel possesses is mind blowing. With my notes, he started to acquire information on the men. He didn't share what he found; just started building file upon file, going in the direction that I hoped would reveal what we needed.

As Diesel worked on Intel, Johnny and Spirit went to get supplies and items from the list Stone put together. Once again, I was not in the loop for that either. All I knew was that the spare shed behind Spirit's torture shed was filling up daily with whatever they were bringing back.

For me, these two weeks allowed me to spend time with Raven, Viola and especially Cari, and Benjamin. I love my sisters, but to have quality time with my children is such a blessing, and something new to me as their mother. There's nothing here to come between us, not even work. So each day I get to know my children and their likes. Ivy had one of my other bakers and cake designers step in, telling them I had a minor surgery and was going to be out for a bit. Stone, or one of the guys, would go to the bakery and pick up all the paperwork, receipts, and supplier forms for me to go over. I would do my fair share to help Ivy and the staff out from here. I know that eventually my presence will be needed, but for now, I'm enjoying life for the first time, with my family.

Stone keeps saying that time is of the essence. From what Diesel's been able to find out, Walker and his minions have gone underground. No one, not even their families, have seen them in the last ten days. This is going to make our plan harder to pull off, but Stone's told me that he's not worried. They have a way to get Walker out of hiding, but I'm not privy to what that information is.

Thinking about Stone has me so fucking confused. Since the night he opened up to me, he's shared other things. Late at night he comes to my room and we just talk, nothing more. It almost feels like he's courting me, which is weird. We're planning on ruining men's lives, and I know that they deserve no pity, but how do we start something when I'm living in my past, every minute of every day? I can't stop myself from fantasizing over Stone. His rugged good looks make my body hum.

My nights after Stone leaves are filled with reading those damn blue journals over and over, reliving all my anger, loneliness, fury, desperation, and hatred. I've tried to use all the tools that the counselors had provided me with, but my head is so fucked up that sleep is not an option right now. If I do fall asleep, the nightmares consume me, putting me back in that loft. I wake up sweating and trembling. My body aches and there's no reason for it, but they're phantom pains.

Fuck, I want this over. I don't know how much more of this I can take.

Feeling a hand on my shoulder, I look up to see Raven standing beside me with a tentative smile on her face. Looking at her breaks my heart. She's lived with her secret for years with no help from anyone, and she's managed someway to continue moving forward.

"Hey, sweetheart, everything okay?"

"Yes, but the kids want to go outside and play. I wasn't sure if that was allowed, so I thought I should ask you first." She squeezes my shoulder. "How are you holding up Quinn? Anything I can do to help? I know you don't trust me right now, but I'm here for you, always. I hope you believe me." As she finishes, her eyes shift to her feet. I can't tell if she's nervous or just not sure how to be around me. My gut tells me to tread carefully with her because of her contact with Walker.

"Raven, why are you so nervous? Are you hiding something from me? Please, don't lie to me. I can see right through you, dear sister. You no longer have that ability to get one over on me."

She smiles sadly.

"No, Quinn. I'm not nervous; I just don't know how to be around you. Truthfully, I'm uncomfortable around you because you seem to have your shit together. Even after everything you've gone through, you're strong and determined. I'm afraid of my own shadow, and now that I've cut Walker completely off, I'm not sure what's going to happen. But it was time. I needed to show all of you that my intentions aren't bad, and that I'm with everyone here. I'm not hiding anything anymore, I swear to God."

"Well, in response to the kids going outside, I don't think it's a good idea unless Johnny or Diesel are with them. I don't want there to even be a chance for Walker or his crew to grab them. They can go out to the screen porch and play a board game if they'd like. Viola will play with them if you don't want to. Just let me know, okay?"

Raven shakes her head and heads to the door. She slowly turns and looks at me intently.

"Quinn, I love you. Always have and always will, no matter what happens. What I did, I thought it was helping keep Walker away from you and the kids. I never, and I mean never, gave him anything that he could use to hurt you. I hope that one day you'll believe me, and I will patiently wait for that day, no matter how long it takes. I miss you."

After she turns and leaves, I contemplate her words. I truly want to believe her, but her actions aren't in line with her comments. All I can do is watch her, then we'll see.

Just as I'm about to go in search of the kids, Stone and the guys come in.

"Quinn, got a minute? I think we're finally ready to share with you our plan." Stone informs me.

"Fuck yeah, I have time. It took you assholes long enough, so fill me in."

CHAPTER 14

We're all sitting around the kitchen table waiting. As I glance at each person here, I realize Spirit's missing, but just as I'm about to ask where she is, I hear Cari come running into the room.

"Momma, Benjamin cheated on the game. Auntie Raven and Auntie Viola are trying to catch him. He got so mad he ran out the house and into the field behind us. Auntie Raven is going nuts back there trying to get to him."

Everyone's up and running out the door before I can say a word to my daughter. She looks around and even at her young age, she realizes something's up. I pull her to me, hugging her tightly.

"Cari, don't worry. Someone will find your silly brother and when they do, I'm going to ground him for being a bad boy. Let's go help."

Walking outside, it looks like a scene from a movie. Some of the guys are running into the field and I can hear both Viola and Raven screaming for Benjamin. Before I realize where everyone else is, Stone and Spirit come riding by us on four-wheelers. Holy shit, this is more than my boy running out after a temper tantrum. They're scared.

Running to the edge of the field I scream at the top of my lungs. "Benjamin Thomas, get your little ass back here immediately. Don't make me come out there to get you."

I feel Cari grab my legs and hold on tight, and then I hear her tiny voice.

"Benji, come on back. I'm not mad. You can say you won. I don't care; I just want you to come back. Benji please, I'm scared."

Feeling my heart pounding in my chest, I hear a noise behind us and see Benjamin coming out of the huge shed behind the house. He's filthy, like he crawled through the mud. He sees us and runs our way just as an SUV comes racing down the dirt road.

I know before I even look that this is not good.

"Stone, there's a car coming this way. Oh my God, please don't be them ... STONE!"

I grab Cari's hand and pull her as I run towards Benjamin. Just as I reach him, the SUV turns towards us and hits the gas. Dirt is flying all over as I quickly look to see that the large shed is our best option. I grab Benji's hand in my other and run, dragging both my children with me. As I clear the door and go to shut it, I realize that whoever is in the SUV is shooting at us. Motherfuckers, not my kids. Looking behind me, I scream, "Go hide behind that container right there and hold on to each other ... go."

They scamper off in the direction I'm pointing to, then I start to pile shit in front of the door. Hearing voices and not sure who they belong to, I continue to pile shit on top of other shit. When I think it's good, I run to my kids and pull them close to me. I kiss their foreheads and quietly tell them,

"Everything is okay, kiddos. Stone will be here shortly so no worries. We're playing hide and seek right now, so we need to be quiet and stay very still. Can you both do that for me?"

All I get are shaky nods, which is fine with me. I don't want them to speak unless it's necessary.

What seems like hours, but I'm sure is only a couple of minutes later, I hear more gunfire, then nothing. Not trusting anything going on, we stay where we are, still as statues.

"Quinn, where the fuck are you sugar? Come on, it's Diesel and me. Give me something, please? Where are you and the children? Fuck, Diesel, was there just the one vehicle? Did they grab them? Fuck, what are we gonna do?"

Once I'm sure it's Stone, I stand up, pulling the kids with me. I go to one of the few windows in this shed and open it.

"Stone, hey, we're here. We're okay, but we need to climb out this way. I blocked the door with a bunch of shit."

Turning, he sees me and the smile he gives me makes my heart beat wildly. He runs towards us, as does Diesel. When they reach us, Diesel immediately reaches up.

"Quinn, give me Benji first. Come on, lil' man, get your ass down here now."

Benji looks scared but does as he's told. He climbs through the window, waits a second before jumping into Diesel's arms. Once he's caught, he puts his head on the big guy's shoulder and starts crying uncontrollably. I'm surprised as hell when Diesel puts a gentle hand on my baby boy's head.

"Benjamin, you're okay. Look at me, lil' man. No one's mad at you. We were just worried, that's all. Come on, show me who's a big guy."

Benji wipes his snotty nose on Diesel's shoulder and looks at him.

"Sorry Diesel. I didn't mean to make so much trouble. I got mad about a silly game we were playing. I'm sorry."

Eyes wet with his tears, my son looks so sorry it breaks my heart. What have I brought my kids into? What happens next tears my heart out.

"Benjamin, you have nothing to be sorry for, son. We all have our moments, and anger can sometimes mess with your head. You have to understand that you and Cari have to be really careful right now. We aren't mad at you and we're just glad you're safe. So no more temper tantrums for the time being, okay? You get me son?"

This comes from Stone who's standing right next to Diesel and Benji. His hand is on my son's back and he's looking Benji in the eyes. After a bit, my son nods and flings himself into Stone's arms, hugging him tightly as Stone returns the hug, holding him sweetly with his eyes closed.

"Come on, Princess, your next. Don't be afraid, Uncle Diesel has your back."

My daredevil daughter doesn't even think, just dives right into Diesel's arms, laughing.

After Stone puts Benji down, he comes under the window.

"Come on, sugar, I got ya. Let's get everyone back in the house. Come on, Quinn, you're wasting time."

I climb through the window and jump, knowing that Stone has me. He always does, and for some reason, I know he always will, no matter what.

As we head back to the house, Stone informs me that he didn't think it was Walker because no one recognized the three guys in the vehicle. They were going to call it in as soon as we got back to the house. Diesel got the plate number, so they'd give that to their guys at the bureau. But to play it safe Stone wanted to move us to another house because even if it wasn't Walker he was worried that this crew might try to come back. So once again we are packing our shit and moving to another house in the country.

CHAPTER 15

After calming down my kids due to not only the recent attack but our move to this new house, I get everyone fed and spend some time with my kids' reading stories before they go off to bed. All the adults are sitting around the kitchen table, and I mean everyone from Stone, his crew, to both my sisters.

Diesel moves file folders in front of him. Pushing some to the left and some to the right, he chooses the one in the middle and opens it. He takes out a few sheets before closing the file back up. He pushes a sheet to me and I grab it. My eyebrows hit my hairline. Holy shit, how the hell did Diesel get all this information? Damn, he's as good as Stone said he is. Diesel starts right in.

"So, after Quinn made the decision on how we were gonna go forward, I started looking into the four assholes, with some of the information she provided. We all kind of know about Walker, but after my research, I can say that we didn't have a clue about this sick pervert here, and the other three also have some serious skeletons in their closets. I've spent the last couple of weeks finding everything I possibly can about Dirk, Marco, and Jazz Man. I will warn ya, it ain't pretty; so let me break it down for ya.

"Quinn's gut was right, at least with Dirk. He's a pedophile and has been for as far back as I can go. He likes young boys. That said, it doesn't mean he won't go for young men, but his candy of choice, his addiction, is boys under ten. I went back through Quinn's notes and once again, she hit it right on. There are boys missing that Dirk coached, and there have been suspicions about his actions over the years, but no evidence or witnesses. Some of the boys quit the teams after their first season with Coach Dirk, but nothing's ever been reported to the police. Something that's interesting is that some of the families of the boys who quit came into some serious cash. Now I'm just assuming, but I think that Walker paid the families off. These parents sold their kids innocence for a payout. Some moved away, while others are still in the same house and the boys are still in school. They don't participate in any after school or sports activities anymore.

"Next is Jazz Man. This is one sick motherfucker, people. Yes, he was the one who caught Kenny's boy, but he also played with him for a while. He tortured and sodomized him before turning him over to Kenny. I think Jazz pushed Kenny into killing his own child. That's just a thought, but knowing Kenny and finding all this shit about Jazz Man, if I had to pick which one was fucked enough to push it, it would be Jazz. He's Walker's right hand and from the report of Quinn's rape, besides Walker, this man was the worst. He took tremendous pleasure in all the pain he inflicted on her."

He lifts his head in my direction before looking back to his papers.

"He's been married and divorced a lot, treating each woman worse than the last. His current wife is much younger, like thirteen years younger, and very naive. Nothing on her except she was actually with Walker first, and now she's with Jazz."

Hearing a gasp, I turn to see Raven with her hand to her mouth, trembling. Tears fill her eyes.

"Raven, honey, what's wrong? Do you know something?"

She shakes her head while wiping her tears. "Walker told me that he breaks the women in, then someone from his crew gets the leftovers. He actually said that to me and laughed about it. He said he wanted to make sure the women had the strength to get through their 'lessons', as he called it. I know he was serious because for some reason, it made him feel powerful telling me this stuff."

Diesel's watching Raven closely, as are Stone and Johnny. After a few moments,

Stone gives a small chin lift and Diesel continues.

"So, like I said, Jazz Man is a sadist, just like Walker. Maybe worse, not sure. They both belong to a BDSM club in the city and consider themselves Masters. Not my thing, but don't believe that culture would allow two assholes to abuse people the way they do, just saying."

I watch as the big man takes a drink of his coffee before finishing it off. "Marco is the last guy. Not sure why he's still part of this crazy bunch because he's the closest to normal as these fucks could be. He's married, has kids, holds a job and lives a relatively normal life. But when Walker calls, he goes to him immediately, which is starting to put a strain between him and the wife. No proclivities to kink, BDSM, or kids, so not sure. Not much else on him, but he's a fucking millionaire. He has more money than the others do, but I don't know how he's gotten to this point. That's what I got so far. I have feelers out for more dirty information, but these guys are careful. We may end up not getting anything else."

Stone stands, reaching for another folder from the pile. He looks at me then gives me one of his sexy smiles.

"We now have background on these guys so we need to move forward and get the plan going. Quinn has written down what she wants to happen to each man, but she's left it up to us as to how we get him to that point. So, let's look over her wishes and see how we can get there with maximum pain to each asshole involved. We'll be saving Walker for last because he won't be able to depend on his 'boys' being there to have his back. This will be a first for Walker, so this should make it interesting. Before we go any further, I want to make it clear that if anyone wants to step away, now is the time. We have been given free reign to get this job done but ya'll know how they operate. I don't want anyone to feel like I'm pressuring you. The choice is yours. I'm all in for Quinn, the kids, and for Viola and Raven. Think about it and know that I won't be angry if anyone decides they want to step back."

All I hear are growls and moans, but Spirit stands so fast, her chair flies back. "Fuck that, Stone. You know we're all in this because of Walker. He's fucked up all of our lives and I for one can't wait to have that motherfucker on my table. The pain I inflict on him will be like nothing he's ever even imagined. No one, and I mean *no one*, is going to keep me from doing to him what I plan to do, so you know I'm in."

The guys just nod as I look on. Feeling eyes on me, I turn and see Stone staring at me. The look in his eyes warms every part of me, including that place between my legs. For some reason he affects me like no other, and always at the most inappropriate times. Looking away, I see everyone watching us. Viola and Raven with smiles on their faces, Diesel and Johnny with smirks, and Spirit with a gentle look in her eyes. I put my head down and wait to hear what's next.

"The plan is spelled out on what's going down. Take the night to look it over, review it and your part in it. If you can come up with anything we missed, let's meet in the morning after breakfast to finalize. We're gonna need to move fast on this before they all disappear and we can't find them. Remember, this is retribution and payback, but it isn't a 'take 'em down' job, unless it's necessary. No one is gonna be killed, got that? Quinn doesn't want anyone put down except for Walker, and when it comes to him, well, we all have a say in his punishment, not just Quinn. He has to go down, there's no question about that. Are we good? If so, let's call it a night. We've had a hell of a day so I hope the night stays quiet. Get some rest everyone."

Stone sits back down, drinking his now lukewarm coffee as everyone stands and goes about their business. I stick around, waiting to see what he has to say to me. I feel the pull that's always around us every time we're together. The electrical current between us could power a small town. The more I learn about Stone, the more I like. He's a good guy who protects the innocent and damaged. Even with everything that happened ten years ago, I can't be mad at him. He's worn me down. I look at him, into those intense green eyes that have haunted me for so many years, and realize I can finally admit that I want him; in any way I can get him.

CHAPTER 16

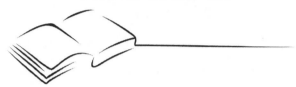

Seeing Quinn looking at me with that look in her eyes immediately sends blood straight to my cock. Fuck, we can't do this now, no matter how much I want to ... no, need to. I've got to stay on point. We're too close to finally finishing this. Just like in her house, I don't want this to be a quick romp in the bed. I've waited too fucking long for that. This woman has driven me crazy with desire, fear, anger, and uncertainty.

"Come on over here, Quinn, and sit down. We need to talk."

Watching her as she approaches, I can see how unsure she is and that tears my heart apart. After all the shit she's gone through, nothing should make her feel insecure or unsure—nothing and no one. As she pulls the chair out next to me, she shifts the chair so it's facing me, then plants her ass into it.

"What's going on in that mind of yours, girl? I can see the wheels turning' and burnin'. Do you feel comfortable with the plan? Anything you want to change or adjust, be honest cause this is the only way that this is gonna work."

I grab her hand and give it a squeeze. As I start to let go, she clutches my hand with both of hers.

"How can I be good with any of this? We're talking about either ruining people's lives, or in Walker's case, ending his permanently. Nothing will ever make this right. It's like we're playing God in a fashion, but I know it needs to be done. There's no choice because if we don't, they'll continue with their sick games. They have no conscience or souls because they torture and kill without a second thought, so no, I'm not good with this, but in my heart I know this is what needs to be done. I've waited too long for this to end with them not paying. I've been re-reading all my blue journals you brought with us. I was immature at first, but the concept is right on. They have to pay for not just me, but for everyone they've hurt. Does that answer your question?"

Nodding, I just look at her. Damn, she's gorgeous, but she also looks exhausted. She needs to get a good night's sleep, without interruptions. Gently releasing her hands, I push up from the chair and go to the furthest cabinet. Grabbing a bottle, I open it, take out a pill and place it back inside the cabinet. Then I grab a water and take both to her. "Sugar, take this. It'll give you a good night's sleep. You're fucking exhausted and need a fresh start. Trust me, I would never give you anything that would hurt you, I swear."

She takes the pill and the water.

"What exactly am I taking? I don't usually take medication so I don't want to take something really strong."

It's just a Valium, something to relax you and not even a high dose. I want you to get some serious rest. You'll thank me."

She looks at the pill one more time before tossing it in her mouth and downing it with the water.

"How long before it kicks in?"

"Usually thirty to forty minutes, but if you don't generally take meds, I would head to bed so you're comfortable when it kicks in. I'll walk you to your room."

We stand and I grab her hand. She doesn't pull away, but instead, she steps closer to me. Wishing her room was across town instead of down the hall, we arrive in no time. Pulling her close, I give her a quick hug.

"Sugar, go on in and sleep. I'll see ya in the morning."

Grabbing me to her, she steps up on her tiptoes and presses her lips to mine for a brief, sweet kiss. I don't dare fucking move.

"Thank you, Stone, for everything. You're a good man. Goodnight."

She then opens the door and enters her room, gently closing the door behind her.

Where did that come from? Feeling like I can't move, I stand there for a couple of minutes, trying to clear my head.

Damn, Quinn never fails to shock the shit out of me, I think to myself as I chuckle. Once I can finally move my feet, I head to my room to get some much-needed shuteye myself.

I wake up in the middle of the night, drenched in my own sweat. That mother fuckin' nightmare is back. Seeing those assholes raping Quinn tears me apart every time. Why is the nightmare coming back to me now? It took years, with the help of counseling and my crew, to finally sleep through the night. But tonight, of all nights, when I really need to have my head in the game, sleep is my enemy. Sitting at the edge of my bed, I run my hands through my soaked hair. This one was really bad. I felt like I was at that window again and couldn't do anything but watch them torture her again and again. My hands are shaking. I get up and leave my room, heading to the kitchen. Maybe I need something to help me sleep too.

Entering the kitchen, I'm shocked to see Raven and Diesel sitting at the table, papers scattered all around them. They both look up at me, startled at my appearance.

"What the hell is going on in here, Diesel?"

"Calm the fuck down, Stone. I couldn't sleep and came in here to get something to drink. Raven was here with all this shit so we've spent the last half hour comparing notes. She knows a lot more about Walker's setup than we even knew. Sit down and check this out."

After a couple of hours, my eyes are dried out and my back has cramps from leaning over the table, going through all the notes. Shit, we should have asked Raven what she knew a long time ago. She's not stupid. She wrote down details of locations, drops, and other things that she saw. She kept her notes hidden so Walker wouldn't find them, but if all this is right, it will help us out tremendously. Fucking Quinn and her sisters, they never cease to amaze me.

As we say our goodnights and head to our rooms, I feel like we're on the right path. I'm so exhausted that by the time I drop my jeans, pull my T-shirt off and yank back the covers, I'm asleep before my head hits the pillow—a deep sleep with no nightmares.

CHAPTER 17

This last month has been fucking intense. After everyone agreed to move forward with the plan, time was of the essence, so we each started getting everything in place. They're all going down and will be punished not only for what they've done to Quinn and others, but also for the way they've lived their lives.

Dirk is the first one on our list. Johnny's been gone for days, trying to get evidence that this asshole is a pedophile and used coaching to find his victims. He located some reports to the police that had been buried under mountains of paperwork.

Diesel's working diligently on the computer to set the plan for when Johnny gets back. Raven's even helping out, keeping everything in order and making sure the timeline is in place. The waiting game is the worst, and it's wearing us down.

Spirit's been following leads on Jazz Man and checking in with all his ex-wives. From the little she's shared, it ain't pretty. The shit that went down with Kenny and his kid was a preview as to how he treated his wives and his own kids. For Spirit to get choked up giving us the information surprised the fuck out of us. She's the toughest person we know, and I'm worried what the hell she found on her searches. The plan for Jazz is going to be difficult because he's the closest to Walker, and we're going to have to grab him the moment we see him. It's getting nerve-racking to say the least.

Marco is going to be the hard one. Quinn is adamant on what she wants us to do with him. Knowing something about Marco that the others don't is becoming harder to keep to myself. They're all confused as to why he doesn't seem like the rest because he doesn't fit the mold of Walker's crew. He has a wife and kids and treats them like gold, works a full-time job, and seems to be a decent person. His only downfall is his work with Walker, and no one knows what their connection is.

Walker is the last one on the list. There's no punishment or torture per Quinn. She wants him killed, simple as that. No dragging it out or making an example of him. Since we have all had our encounters with Walker throughout the last fifteen plus years, it is unanimous that Walker dies.

The people Walker and his deceased father, Marty, associated with are just as sick of Walker as we are. Even more so because he's not his father. Marty held a tight leash on every aspect of the business. Walker has no idea who, what, or where to go to keep things running smoothly. Besides that, he's a psychopath who likes to torture, rape, and murder women, and we need to put a stop to it."

Hearing someone approaching, I turn to see Quinn walking my way with two bottles of water in her hands.

"Hey, got a minute? If so, can we take this outside? I want to talk to you about something."

Following her out the side door, my eyes drift to her heart shaped ass and my cock hardens, just like every time we're together. I'm so tired of beating off at night in my room with all the snapshots in my mind of her. No matter what she's doing, if I see it, my dick gets hard. And to top that off, I'm trying to be a gentleman. Yeah, that's a fucking joke. The guys are ramming it up my ass 'cause that word and me have no affiliation, until now.

Bringing my attention to the now, I see Quinn sitting at the picnic bench, waiting for me to join her. Shit, I gotta quit getting caught up in my head.

"So, what's up, sugar? Everything okay?"

"Yeah, everything is good, just need you to help me get my head right. Since we're in hiding, or whatever you call it, I can't talk to my therapist, so maybe you can help me. Like you said, the guilt is starting and we haven't even done anything yet. I'm sleeping with that pill every night but whenever I'm awake, the guilt weighs me down. How do I live with myself after we finally finish this shit? How do you process all that you do in your job every day? Please, can you help me?"

Pulling her to me, I wrap my hand around her waist and give it to her straight.

"I told you I won't ever lie to you. It's never easy. There are some cases that still to this day haunt me, and yours is one of them. But I try to separate the good and bad from each case and how we helped the victim. Hang on a minute. Let me grab my laptop. I want to show you something."

Jogging to my bedroom, I grab the laptop and shuffle back outside. Opening it up, I find the file I want to show her and wait for it to load.

"Quinn, these pictures are graphic. They're from the night of your attack."

She gasps, so I slowly rub my hand up and down her back.

"If you think you can look at these, maybe it will push that guilt right out of your head. Do you feel like you can handle looking at them? If you can't, don't worry about it, but this is the best way I can try to help you."

Watching her struggle with the idea of seeing things she'd rather forget, I wait patiently. This is her decision and all I can do is support her with whatever she decides.

After what seems like hours, but is only minutes, she makes her decision.

"Show me."

I nod and hit enter on the keyboard, then turn the screen to her. "This is what I did to make what happened to you make some sense. I'm not minimizing the hell they put you through, but this tells your story, Quinn."

I hear the music start and know the slideshow has started. I hear her once again draw in a deep breath, so I reach around her, placing my arm around her shoulders, and pull her into my side. Together we watch the video, each of us reliving a night that never should have happened. The one night that for us forever changed our paths in life. A change orchestrated by a sadist.

CHAPTER 18

After watching the slideshow with Stone, I needed some time alone. The raw feelings running through my body and soul left me with no words to explain to him what exactly I was feeling, so I retreated to my room.

Now its days later and I can't seem to leave my bed. I feel beaten, extremely emotional, and lost. The only people that have been in here are the children and Viola. No matter what, my kids always have access to me and I have to be there for them. They don't get what's going on, and trying to keep them entertained is so hard.

Viola came in because she knew that something was going on. Dealing with her own emotional issues, she gets it, and more importantly, she doesn't push or prod. She's here to let me cry in her arms, giving me emotional support, and just being Viola.

By day three, the feelings coming from outside the room are crawling under the door, reaching for me. Knowing that my time in here is coming to an end, I get out of bed and go to the bathroom. Damn, I need a shower. I can smell my own stink. I open the shower door and turn on the water. I enter and just stand under the spray, letting the hot steamy water relax my tense body. Going through my routine, I finally open the door and let out a loud scream as a towel is pushed into my face.

"Jesus Christ, what the hell? You scared the fucking shit out of me. What's your problem?"

"My problem? Really? You've been holed up in your room, talking to no one, seeing no one. I asked you if you were ready to see it, knowing it was extreme, but you can't hide anymore. You asked for us to help you, and that's what we're doing, but you need to be with us."

Wrapping the towel tightly around me, I grab Stone's hand and lead him through to the bedroom. Getting us situated on the edge of the bed, I gather my thoughts before speaking.

"The slideshow did bother me, but not like you think, and bother is the wrong word. I was so overwhelmed by what you put together. I saw the journey of my life from that point on, and you concentrated not on the negative, but the positive. You blew me away and emotionally ripped me to shreds. Never has anyone gone to that much trouble for me. I know it was your catalyst to help you, but to me it's everything."

I look at her face and I'm shocked. I watch a small smile appear on her lips as tears roll down her cheeks. Her eyes never leave mine as her hand travels up my arm to my face. She moves to wrap her hands around my neck, and pulls me towards her face.

"I need you to kiss me, Stone … please?"

She doesn't have to ask me twice. I lean in and very gently touch my lips to hers. The feeling is mind blowing. It's pure, hot, and so damn good. Not wanting to go too far or push her too much, I grasp her head in my hands, turning her head the way I want it to get better access. Once there, I lick her bottom lip with my tongue and her mouth opens for me. My tongue delves into hers and the temperature in the room increases immediately. We fight for control with teeth, lips, and tongues, dueling for more. As Quinn finally pulls away, gasping for air, I hold her close, giving her light kisses all over her lips, face, eyes, and back to her lips again. Needing to taste her one more time, my open lips hit hers as my tongue immediately pushes in to taste what is all Quinn. My jeans are fucking straining as my cock fights to bust through my zipper. Swear to God, the teeth of the zipper are going to leave imprints on my dick, I'm so hard.

I hear Benjamin and Cari running down the hall. Trying to catch my breath, I close my eyes to try and center myself. Obviously, it doesn't fucking work because Benjamin asks me, "What's wrong, Stone? Why are you breathing so hard? Your face looks funny too. Are you sick?"

Quinn laughs under her breath. "What's up, my loves? Did you need something from me?"

"Mom, we need you to come to the kitchen. Lunch is ready and Spirit told us to let you know and these aren't her exact words, but she said,

"Tell your momma if her butt isn't out here, I'm coming to get her and she won't like it."

Suddenly, laughter fills the room. I see Quinn giggling like a little girl as her kids begin pulling her by her arms, out of the room towards the kitchen. Looking over her shoulder, she looks me up and down and her eyes go wide. She puts the brakes on, informing her children she needs to get dressed first. As she turns, the hungry look she gives me makes my dick stand at attention yet again. Then with a sexy grin, she winks and disappears into the bathroom to get dressed.

CHAPTER 19

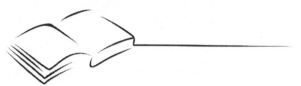

During lunch, I can feel the tension in the room. Spirit, Johnny, and Diesel keep looking back and forth between each other. Viola senses this and takes the kids to the family room to watch a movie. As soon as they leave, Johnny starts in.

"Here it is. We've been waiting for one of these jag bags to make an appearance. Well, one did and did it big. Just got word that Dirk is up and you won't believe where they found him. I know we've heard that there are those clubs where perverts go to get their kink on for a price. That is where he was spotted.

Johnny glares as both Spirit and Diesel laugh out loud.

"Johnny my man don't get all pissed off not talking about your kind of club ok? Diesel grunts between laughs.

"Fuck you, *brother*. Don't act like you're an innocent 'cause remember I know your type of club too." Johnny fires back.

I see the difference in Diesel as his anger fills his features. He stares at Johnny with a look that would scare just about anyone in its path.

"Let's drop this conversation for another time when we can really dive into each other's unique preferences. For now let's stay focused on the job at hand. And just sayin dude my connections due to my special likes is what opened doors to finding Dirk."

Johnny nods but says nothing. He knows he fucked up, but Johnny being Johnny, walks over to Diesel, placing his hand on the big man's arm.

"Dude, no disrespect meant. I apologize. This shit is taking its toll, but there's no excuse for what I said. We're brothers, and I don't care what you do in your personal time. I was just pulling your chain."

As the two of them settle down, I feel someone watching me. I turn to see Raven with her eyes intent and focused on me. Not knowing why, I glance at Quinn, who's watching the interaction between the guys. I look back and give Raven a questioning look, but she shakes her head and holds up one finger.

I turn back to the group and listen intently as Johnny continues

"Dirk showed up at one of the closed clubs that we hear about, but no one knows where they meet or who they are. But one of our informants specifically stated that he saw Dirk there. Not gonna go into details, but this motherfucker is a sick asshole, Stone. This is our time to grab him and take him down. He'd never think we'd find him there so he's feeling safe. Let's break that safety net and send him to hell."

Raven is still standing there, watching everyone intently, so I finally have to ask. "Raven, do you know something?"

For the first time ever, I see her temper as she glares at me, then she shakes her head and gives it to me.

"Yes, I'm very interested in what's being said. This is our life and what happens can cause blowback on us. Quinn has been through enough, and we need to protect Cari, Benjamin, and Viola. I'm racking my brain, trying to figure out all the stuff I've heard over the years, and I want to make sure if there's something that can help you guys, that I tell you. I have no hidden agenda, and seeing the way you're looking at me, I know you don't believe me. Truthfully, I don't care if you do or not. Anything else?"

Studying Raven, I'm looking for any signs of her trying to play us, but I don't see anything.

Johnny and Diesel continue to go back and forth between the computer and the notes scattered around the table, then shocking us all, Raven speaks up.

"I knew that place they hung out was sick. It's an old warehouse on South Street, and it always smelled like a mix of bleach, vomit, and urine. That has to be where he's taking the kids, right? I never saw anyone, but that doesn't mean they weren't there. The more I think about it, that place is perfect for them to take someone without anyone ever knowing. Stone, you have to check it out. I've been there, it's the truth. When I was still trying to keep Walker away from Quinn and Viola, that's where he would tell me to meet him. As scared as he made me, I wanted to see if I could find something … anything, to stay one step ahead of him so he couldn't hurt my family any more than he already has. All these years, I thought I was doing the right thing, thinking I was keeping him away, but I've only made things worse. I know this now."

Diesel's already on his phone. I hear his conversation, giving directions to where the warehouse is located. He's probably talking to one of the field guys, and Diesel's right to have them go check it out first. I'm still not sure if we can trust Raven or not. She's stayed in contact with Walker all this time, like nothing he's done ever happened. I don't understand her reasoning for it, but I need to get her side of the story. I guess I can understand it to a point. She thought she was doing it for all the right reasons, and people do crazy things when they're scared.

Johnny's asking Raven all kinds of questions about the location, so I take a minute and go over to Quinn, who seems to be falling asleep at the table.

"Sugar, why don't you go to bed? We're going to be a while, checking some things out. Nothin' you can do here right now, so get some rest. The kids are gonna be a handful again tomorrow so take some time for you."

She raises her eyes to me, but says nothing. Watching her watch me, I get the feeling something is changing in the way she views me. Not sure what's caused it, but I'm sure as hell not complaining.

"I want to stick around and hear what you find out, especially about what Raven's shared. Do you believe her, Stone, or is she trying to lead us into a trap? I don't know what to believe, or if I can even trust her. How do you do this all the time? It's driving me nuts. We need this to end once and for all."

I pull her to me and give her a much-needed hug. She reacts by putting her hands around my back and holding on tight. We stand there, just hugging and giving each other comfort, until Diesel yells out, "Fuck, the guys just did a drive-by and Dirk's there. They saw him dragging in a kid around ten or eleven, half-conscious. Stone, this is it. It's fucking go time, right the fuck now."

CHAPTER 20

After begging Stone to let me come, we all pile into the SUV and race to the location. Watching them work together, I can see they're in their element.

"Quinn, I want you to stay behind me at all times. If I tell you to do something, you do it without question. You got me, sugar?"

Nodding, I follow him to the side entrance. They signal to each other, and Diesel uses some type of gun that blows the door wide open. Immediately I hear screams for help. Stone grabs my hand and puts it through the loop of his belt.

"Do not let go or leave my back, no matter what you see."

He knows that this is gonna be bad. Even though the team has shared with me, I kind of knew they were keeping some of the graphic shit to themselves. Well, if I'm ever going to move forward, I need to suck it up and deal with whatever falls my way.

Just as we turn the corner, I get a glimpse of Spirit running into a room, gasping and screaming at the top of her lungs.

"You sick motherfucker. This is the last fucking time you ever hurt a kid. I swear to God, you bastard, if you don't step away from him I will shoot you between the eyes. And just so you know, I never miss, so step the fuck away now!"

Walking through the door, my stomach clenches and I feel the vomit rushing up my throat. The poor child has snot running down his nose, his cheeks are bright red and wet from crying. I can't begin to describe the horror of what I'm seeing before me. The young boy appears to be in shock from the atrocities he has been through.

His eyes lock onto mine before moving to Diesel who makes his way slowly and carefully towards the boy. As the boy starts to back up, Diesel quietly speaks to him while putting his arms out in front of him, hands up. I can hear Diesel's words to the boy.

"Don't worry, lil' man, I won't let anyone hurt you again. I swear you're safe with us. Hearing Diesel comforting the young boy I finally come to accept that Stone's crews are good people who really care about the faceless victims of society. After the last sentence, the boy lets out a huge sob before running into Diesel's huge arms. Watching both boy and man comforting each other is heartbreaking. Diesel picks up the young boy like he weighs nothing, covers him with his coat and leaves the building.

Turning, I see Stone push past Spirit, going right for Dirk, punching him square in the center of his face. Dirk's nose explodes with blood as he howls in pain. By the time Stone throws him to the floor, Spirit's there, grabbing his head and pounding it into the concrete floor. The constant pounding of Dirk's head on the floor is making me ill.

"Stop, Spirit, you're gonna kill him. Come on, we agreed his punishment should be jail so he gets the same shit he's given these kids. He'll pay every day of his miserable life so please, Spirit, don't do this."

I'm begging for her to not kill a fucking pedophile, but we talked about each punishment, and for Dirk, prison would be the perfect punishment for him. Stone let it be known and spread the word about Dirk's obsession with raping young boys. As sick as it makes me, thinking of what will happen to Dirk, in that dark recess of my soul, I know it's what Dirk deserves. He actually deserves worse.

Spirit moves away from Dirk and we all circle around him. Groaning and moaning, he attempts to get up a couple times before succeeding. When he finally gets a glimpse of me standing behind Stone, he let's loose.

"*You.* This is all because of you, you fucking bitch. I told Walker years ago to get rid of you, but he wouldn't listen. Never understood his fascination with you, his obsession. So, does it feel good, Quinn, knowing that you managed to get to me with their help?" He nods towards Stone, Johnny, and Spirit.

"You piece of shit. You're nothing but a Goddamn coward. Any man who beats and rapes women and children is nothing but an insecure fuckwad. Your problem is that you have little dick syndrome. Yours was the only one I didn't even feel, so that's why you needed to be so rough, right? Don't worry, you'll never get to fuck anyone else again because you'll be too busy getting fucked by some of the biggest dicks in prison. We've made sure that they know you're coming, and you know how prisoners feel about raping children, don't ya? They're all drooling, waiting for your ass to be theirs, but for one in particular, it's personal and close to home.

"You have a 'signature' you like to leave your victims with, right? Yeah, we know about it. Each child you've victimized over the years had one thing in common. That's the way you leave them to be found after you're done. Even though half of them are way too gone to give the authorities any assistance, you've gotten sloppy and the last few have given partial descriptions. How does it feel now, knowing you'll spend the rest of your life being another man's bitch? Think on that as they're getting you ready for transport. I hope they fuck you good and proper, asswipe. You will live the nightmare you brought to your young victims every moment you are in prison. That is your just reward."

Watching Quinn break Dirk down is the best sight I've ever seen. Each sentence gives back to her the confidence these animals stole from her so many years ago. I'm so proud of her for being strong and accepting the things that need to be done. She's becoming who she needs to be.

"Hey, can't we talk ... make a deal? I can give you what you really want, Quinn. I can lead you straight to Walker. He's the one who started all this and ruined your life. Get your *friend* over there to come talk to me. I'll give you shit that will give you nightmares for the rest of your life. The things we've done—you have no idea. Oh shit, you probably don't know about the holding house, or as we call it, the Laboratory. If you work with me, you might be able to save the ones still there, but I'm warning you, Quinn. It's not a place you want to go into. You'll never be the same. You thought what happened to you was bad, you have no fucking idea what pain and suffering really is." Dirk finishes on a laugh and stares at all of us, waiting. Knowing that Stone and his crew's jobs are to save lives, I start to worry about Dirk getting out of his punishment. My hands start to sweat and shake as I watch Spirit and Johnny give each other a strange look.

Feeling Stone's hands on my shoulders, he leans in and quietly whispers, "Quinn, you need to leave, right now. Go to the SUV and lock yourself inside. Listen to the radio. I'll be out shortly."

Knowing this isn't a request, I turn and start to walk out, but before I exit, I turn to face Dirk and with a smirk on my face, I finally let his part in my past go.

"No matter what happens, Dirk, I know Stone won't turn you free so either you spend it as someone's bitch in jail, or you'll be six feet under. Either way, I'll sleep in peace knowing you're no longer a threat. Have a great life, asshole ... *NOT.*"

CHAPTER 21

Waiting for Stone and the others to finish whatever it is they're doing with Dirk, I try to stop the violent shakes running through my body. Man, did I put on a great show before walking out of that building, but that was what it was—a show. Now I'm having an anxiety attack as my heart pounds out of my chest, and sweat falls down my forehead. I can't get rid of this overwhelming feeling of impending doom. Suddenly, a squad and undercover cars, as well as a huge van, surround the building with SWAT on the side. Holy shit, what the fuck is going on? Are Stone and the guys okay? Shit, Spirit's still in there too. I don't know what to do. Do I stay in the SUV, or go see if I can help in any way?

Before I can come to a decision, the driver's side door opens and Spirit jumps in, smiling. The back doors then open as Diesel and Johnny hop in too.

"Where's Stone? Is he ok? Come on, guys, don't leave me hanging. What's going on with Dirk?"

Spirit answers. "That asshole is trying to cut a deal for himself—not for his family or his brood of kids to keep them safe. All he's concerned about is himself. Johnny knocked out two of his teeth. Fucking pisses me off that he thinks he can give up Walker and get out of any prison time. Do we look stupid? He's going to fucking pay for what he's done, one way or another."

Her last comment gets me a long stare before she looks out the window.

"This shit is coming close to the end and I'm proud of ya girl for staying strong. I'm telling you this because things are going to get complicated and you need to stay the course. We're down to two now, so keep doing what you're doing Quinn."

With her intensity, all I can do is nod. Sometimes she frightens me more than the guys do.

Diesel gives me a sad smile. "Lil' man is on his way to the hospital. Hopefully he'll be okay with time and some help."

That poor child is lucky we got here in time.

"Take us back home, Spirit. Stone said he'll catch us later," Johnny says.

"Is it safe to leave him alone," I ask

"Quinn, he can handle just about anything, so don't worry. Let's move." As we drive back to the safe house, my mind is all over. Why would Stone want to stay behind? What was going to happen to Dirk and how badly injured is he? Will Walker figure it out, that we have one of his men and that we're coming for him too? I'm so overwhelmed that I don't even notice that we are at the house. Shit, talk about scatterbrained. Getting out of the SUV, I see the kids running to me.

"Momma, where have you been? We've been hiding like Auntie Viola told us to. Where is she? Momma, come on, we need to find her."

Immediately I feel a chill run down my spine. What do the kids mean that Viola isn't here? Where the fuck are Raven and Viola? We moved to this new safe house to prevent Walker from finding us. What the fuck is going on.

"Let's go inside and sit down. Come on, kids, let's get in the house now."

Diesel's on his phone as Johnny and Spirit are looking in the other buildings. I get the children in the house and sit them at the kitchen table and I start to fix them a snack. I'm trying not to let them know how scared I am for Viola. She isn't the type to go off on her own, so something is definitely wrong. Just as I place some cut up fruit and juice out for my children, I hear Johnny screaming my name. Looking at the kids, I say, "Stay in this house and lock the door behind me. No questions, just please do as I ask. Diesel is here so listen to him."

I run out the door, hearing the lock click into place. Listening for Johnny's voice, I continue running to the farthest building. He's pacing in front of the place, rubbing his hands back and forth through his hair. Lifting his head, he looks at me with such pain in his eyes I instantly stop.

"What is it Johnny? Is it Viola? Please tell me it isn't her." When he doesn't answer, I scream, "Fucking tell me, Johnny."

"Quinn, honey, it's not Viola in there, it's Raven. I won't lie; it's bad ... she's really bad off. We called an ambulance, but she wants you."

Pushing past him, I trip through the door and my eyes drift to the shape on the floor. Raven's lying there, spread eagle on the floor, hands and legs restrained by ropes tied to the posts in the room. She's naked and beaten black and blue. Her eyes are swollen shut and she's bleeding everywhere. I run to my sister and gently touch her swollen cheek.

"Honey, Raven, its Quinn. I'm here now. Raven, I'm here."

She tries to open her eyes, but after much effort, she just lets out a breath of frustration.

"They didn't get her, Viola. She's in the old bomb shelter behind the house. I shoved her in and locked it before they could see her. She's safe, Quinn. I swear to God, she's safe."

With tears running down my face, I hold her hand, telling her it will be all right, but I'm not sure if it's true.

"Raven, who did this? Why didn't you go into the shelter too? Shit. Johnny, Viola's in the bomb shelter. Please, get her out."

Raven shakes her head violently.

"Quinn I told the kids to hide in that room Stone showed us. The secret room behind the closet they had prepared just in case. God please tell me they are ok. I can't even breathe if they aren't. Quinn the kids are ok right?"

Hearing Raven moan, I realize how bad she's hurt. Not knowing what to do, I look over my shoulder to see Spirit enter with a huge first aid kit in her hands.

"Raven, its Spirit. Where do you hurt? Talk to me, sweetie. Let me help you."

As Spirit asks the questions, her hands run up and down Raven's body. From her reactions, when Spirit's hands hit Raven's ribs, I assume they're broken. She has deep cuts on her body, along with bruising on her face. Spirit gives me a knife.

"Cut her loose, then gently move her arms and legs together so she isn't stretched out like this."

Doing what she asks, I cut the ropes, which have dug into Raven's skin, tearing it apart. Very carefully, I move her arms first, to her dismay, then her legs. When I push her legs together, I see for the first time blood is pooling under her ass. It seems to be coming from her vagina. Fuck, they raped her too.

Spirit catches my eyes and looks to Raven. I get that she wants me to move. Once out of her way, Spirit gently touches Raven's stomach and then goes down. The instant she touches her pelvic area, Raven screams out. Spirit immediately steps back.

"Raven, honey, can you let Spirit check you out? She knows what she's doing?"

Shaking her head, she tries to talk but struggles for a few minutes before revealing the horror she's been put through.

"Quinn, don't let her touch me, not there. They raped me with a bottle and I think there's glass inside of me. It hurts so bad, Quinn. Please don't touch me, please."

The horror shows on both Spirit's face and mine.

"Who did this Raven? Were you able to see their faces?"

She struggles to swallow, but gets it out. "Walker ... it was Walker."

CHAPTER 22

In the last three weeks, Dirk was sent to a maximum-security prison with no trial. His justice was swift, due to our connections. No one else has been seen or heard from since.

Raven is recovering slowly. Her injuries were bad, but she's back at home now, the third safe house we've been moved to now. Viola hasn't left her side, and neither have the kids. She's being waited on hand and foot, to her dismay. This includes Diesel too, whenever he's around. It's actually cute to see the two of them together. It's obvious that he cares for my sister.

Dirk hasn't fared so well. After he was sent to the federal prison and put in general population, his luck ran out. Somehow his prior activities were revealed, and according to Stone's contact, Dirk is being treated as one of the prison bitches, being shared and used the same way he did to all those young children over the years. Dirk doesn't seem to be enjoying his new friends too much, as he's tried to kill himself numerous times in the last week. He's in isolation for now, receiving medical treatment for his injuries. Stone told me that he's been begging to see me, but we all know that isn't going to happen. What goes around, comes around, and it's Dirk's time to learn that.

As far as Jazz Man and Marco, no one knows where those two are. Stone, Johnny, and Diesel have been spending days at a time, trying to find a lead, but they've gotten nothing. It's like they've disappeared into thin air. Walker either helped them leave the country, or he buried them in the country. Either way, all we can do is sit and wait.

Walker hasn't been out in public either. There have been some sightings of him, but nothing leading to his capture. I'm getting impatient and pissed off. How much longer do we have to stay here? I've been checking in with Ivy regarding the bakery, but haven't been there in forever. One of my assistants has stepped up to help with all the baking, decorating, and making sure everything is handled.

Just as I'm preparing lunch for everyone, my cell rings. Not recognizing the number, I answer it tentatively.

"Hello."

"Hello, Quinn. How are you?" Walker's voice comes across the line.

How is it possible the one time he contacts me, I'm alone?

FUCK!

"What do you want? You have some fucking nerve calling me. I can't wait to end you, motherfucker."

I'm just about to hang up until I hear him say, "Before you go, there's someone who wants to say something to you. Hang on a minute." I hear some noise in the background and almost drop the phone when I hear a voice I know, sounding defeated.

"Quinn, don't do anything he tells you to, no matter what. Ouch, asshole, that fucking hurt."

I hear a slap then another and another till Ivy goes quiet. I hear a thump and Walker is back on the phone.

"Quinn, you have two hours to get the Goddamn computer Dad used and get your ass to the bakery. Otherwise, you might not recognize Ivy when you see her next. Oh, and by the way, you should be receiving a surprise delivery about now. You wanted Jazz Man, so I sent him to you."

I hear Walker laughing hysterically and psychotically before the phone goes dead. Before I can think, I hear Viola screaming and Raven crying. I run to the family room of the house and see my sisters hugging each other tight, looking at a shipping box sitting in the middle of the room. Something tells me not to look, not even for a second, but then I know I need to see what's in the box. Both girls are hysterically crying and moving away from it, so I make my way towards them first.

"Are you both okay? What is it, tell me..."

Neither one speaks, but Raven points towards the box.

I step to it and move the one lip so I can see inside. What I do see will never leave my mind for as long as there is breathe in me. Walker didn't lie, he sent me Jazz Man, in pieces.

In the box is the body of Jazz Man, cut up into multiple pieces with his head on top, eyes looking blankly at me from the pile beneath him. All I can do is stare, then the most horrified scream starts deep in my gut and makes it way out of my mouth. I don't even recognize the sound, but I can't seem to stop it. I hear footsteps running down the hallway and realize I don't want my children to see this. I turn to tell Viola, but she's already running out of the room.

"Come on, Cari and Benjamin. Let's go back to your room."

"But Auntie Viola, that's our momma. What's wrong with her? We need to help her." I hear my daughter plead.

"Kids, listen to your aunt and one of us will be in shortly."

This comes from Stone and I know the kids will listen to him, just like I've started to. He enters the room and looks in the box, then closes it and looks over his shoulder.

"Get this shit out of here. Don't care what ya do with it, just move this motherfucker out of the house. Quinn, come here now," he barks. I walk to him as he pulls me tight and just holds me against him. It allows me to calm down and find my center in this nightmare that never seems to end.

"Stone, right before I heard the girls, Walker called my cell. He has Ivy at the bakery and demanded that I come there with my dad's computer. He was beating on her and I could hear it over the phone. We have to get her away from him before he ruins her like he did me and Raven."

Suddenly he grabs me by the arms and looks at me. "You are not ruined. Don't ever say that again. You are the strongest person I know, and we'll get Ivy to safety. This is it

for Walker because his time has come.
Don't worry about it, Quinn, we got this, I
swear."

CHAPTER 23

After spending around twenty minutes trying to get a plan in place, Stone finally gives the go ahead for all of us to head to the bakery. Grabbing my hand, he holds me close until everyone else heads out the door. Viola's staying back with the kids, along with two guys Stone says he's worked with before.

"Sugar, I need a minute, okay? Gotta say this before we go get Ivy back and take care of Walker for good. I know you're scared and don't trust me all the way yet. I need you to know how much these last couple of months of us getting to know each other have helped me too, Quinn. I feel like you truly know me now, and how much you mean to me. I just want to say that when this is over, I want you to give us a chance.

All I'm askin' for is a chance. You have owned my heart since that night ten years ago, and no matter what or who has been in my life since then, they've only been distractions. Sorry to say that, that's what they were until I could build up the courage to get what was mine, and that's always been you, and only you. So don't think we're beaten and Walker has the upper hand. What pushes me is that at the end of the day, I get to see you and spend time with you and the kids. That in itself is the best gift on this earth. So, we've gotten through your past and we're working through your present. I'm hoping to have a spot in your future."

He looks down on me and slowly lowers his head, gently pressing his lips to mine. I open my mouth and kiss him back, telling him everything that I haven't said in words. When we finally separate to catch our breaths, I smile at him for the first time, all my emotions on my face.

"Stone, I know that you've always had my back, even that night. It's going to take me some time to appreciate that I have a future to look forward to, so let's get through this today and then we can talk about the future and what it holds for us. Today we get our lives back, and hopefully Walker goes to jail, or loses his life. So, my badass protector, let's get this party started."

Driving to Sweet Bits & Pieces Bakery, the SUV is quiet. Quinn, Johnny, and I are in one vehicle while Diesel and Spirit are in the other car, following us but not too closely. We don't want to freak Walker out with Ivy in his clutches. I can tell Quinn is about to lose it by her body language. Her legs are bouncing up and down with nervous energy while she wrings her hands in her lap. Reaching over the console, I grab her hands, pulling them apart. Keeping one in my hand, I squeeze it then place it on her lap, trying to stop her from bouncing.

"We got this, Quinn. Have some faith. Too much time has already gone by and we'll not let you down. It's time to get your life back, no matter what that life is. You hear me, sugar?"

She nods slowly and I can feel her gaze on me. Johnny leans forward, touching her shoulder and gently squeezes it.

"Girl, I will tell you that this man here would go to the ends of the earth to protect you and make sure nothing happens to you and your family. Remember what Stone said; trust us. Nothing is gonna go wrong, we all promise."

I look in the rear view mirror as I see Diesel and Spirit following us, knowing they're all in too. We've been working too long on this one to let anything go wrong. We've got this, I just know it.

With traffic, it takes an extra ten minutes or so to arrive at the bakery. Parking in the back, I go around the SUV to help Quinn down while Johnny, gun at the ready, emerges from the back seat. I pull out my own gun and prepare myself as we each take a side next to Quinn, as we slowly walk to the employee entrance in the back. Before we get there, the door flies open and I swing my gun up. Walker is standing there, holding an assault rifle, pointing it directly at Quinn with a crazy, sick smile on his face. What alarms me and draws a gasp from Quinn is the blood covering his T-shirt, hands, and jeans.

Knowing this isn't going to be easy, I prepare for what we're about to walk into. I push her behind me, but not before whispering quietly, "Prepare yourself. Try not to show any emotion, as he will feed off of it. No matter what's happened to Ivy, we'll help her."

"Stone, I may have survived, but until you came into my life, I never really thought about living. You did that. Now, let's get Ivy."

We turn to Walker and he moves to the side, all of us aiming our firearms at one another as we walk past him, into who fucking knows what.

CHAPTER 24

Walking through the hallway, I can feel the panic setting in. I have Stone in front of me, Johnny behind me, and Walker bringing up the rear. I know that no matter what I see, I won't be prepared for it. Walker is fucking crazy, and looking for shock value. As we walk past the kitchen, everything looks normal. Continuing past my office, there's nothing there either. The bathroom door is slightly closed, but we hear a muffled sound coming from behind it. Watching Stone move, he pushes the door open. I hold back the scream that's stuck in my throat. On the floor are two of my employees, tied up and beaten badly. One is a teenage boy named Jimmy who helps with the cleaning of the bakery. The other is my designer, Dorothy, who has taken my place during all this.

She's a middle-aged woman with a family. They both look like hell.

Jimmy's face looks like hamburger meat, while Dorothy looks to be in shock. She's naked from the waist down, and I can't even look because at first glance, her thighs are glistening with semen. *Son-of-a-bitch*. This asshole just doesn't stop.

Johnny pushes past us to check them out, pulling the messenger bag off his shoulder. He immediately takes a syringe out and gives Jimmy something, hopefully for his pain, then removes his hoody and covers Dorothy up with it. He checks her pulse and digs in his bag, pulling out, of all things, a Gatorade.

"Here, darlin', drink this for me, will ya?"

Dorothy's head shoots up and looks at Johnny hesitantly, then over us to Walker. There's so much fear in her eyes, I want to take the gun that Johnny has put down and kill Walker myself, once and for all.

She finally takes the drink after Johnny opens it for her. She gingerly brings it to her lips, taking a sip, then another. She then passes it to Jimmy, holding it for him as Johnny holds his head.

Walker's had enough and barks out, "Are you here to rescue the help or give me what I want and get your friend, Quinn? Let's move, I don't have all fucking day."

Stone gives Johnny a chin lift and walks past Walker, who follows us, his gun to my back.

When we enter the main bakery, I can't believe my eyes. Oh my God, Ivy ... I think? Before I can even take in her condition, I see that Walker has covered the two huge storefront windows with newspapers, and pulled the blinds down on the door and side glass. Hate runs through my veins. I turn to Walker, asking him what's bothered me for years.

"Why, Walker? What did I ever do to you for you to hate me so much to not only ruin my life, but all the others you've tortured, murdered, and fucked up? Are you that crazy? Make me understand?"

He turns to me and for once, his eyes look at me confused for a brief second, then he shuts down and stares back at me.

"Quinn, I don't hate you, never have. You're family, so why would you think that? I wanted to make our parents suffer for how they'd treated me, but you had to step in and try to save their sorry asses, and in front of my crew nonetheless. Couldn't let you off, so I had to set an example. You weren't a virgin, so quit crying like you were. Try and tell me you didn't like some of it. Go ahead, play the martyr."

I stare at him in shock. Is he serious? What the fuck is wrong with him.

"Walker, you fucking asshole. I didn't *enjoy* being raped, beaten, and humiliated. My life stopped that night and I've just existed for years. So, to answer your fucked up question … no, I didn't enjoy any portion of it. Not one bit."

"Really? Not even Romeo over there watching through the window? Think I didn't see you, Stone? I knew for a while you had the hots for Quinn, so I needed to put you in your place. She would never be yours, and she never will be." He pauses and looks between Stone and I before he continues. "Well, it's been great going down memory lane, but let's get down to business. I don't know how much longer Ivy over there can hang on."

I go to move towards her, but Walker steps up and pulls me back. I lose my balance and if not for Stone, I would have fallen right into one of the bakery glass cases. Stone lets out a growl, but I grab his hand, keeping him close to me while he holds his gun on Walker with the other.

I look at Ivy. She's hanging with her hands tied above her head, the rope wrapped around the main beam. She's barely able to touch the ground, she's strung so tight. Her clothes are off and there isn't a part of her gorgeous body that isn't marked, bruised or bitten. On the inner part of her thigh is the "W" brand, but there's no number yet. The only part not touched is her face, which looks strange compared to her beaten and bruised body. Her head is leaning to the side, drool running out of her mouth and down her chin. Her eyes are semi-closed with tears running down her cheeks. I'm not sure if she's been raped or not. I continue to look her way until her eyes open. She tries to give me a smile, but she's too weak.

Fuck, we need to get her cut down and to the hospital. What are we waiting for? Turning to Stone, I beg him with my eyes, letting him know that we need to take care of Ivy, and quick.

"So, Quinn, did you bring the laptop like I told you to? Cause if you didn't, we have a serious problem. Is it in the bag Romeo's hanging onto? Throw the bag here, Stone ... now."

Stone doesn't move or make any inclination that he's going to obey the request, so Walker starts to head to where Ivy is hanging. I can't help it, I let out a loud screech.

"Walker, please, leave her alone. Hang on a minute."

"Quinn, darling sister. Nothing against you, but if that asshole is going to play games, then games it is."

He reaches out to the table beside Ivy and pulls up a scary looking whip like thing. I'm unsure of what it is exactly, but as soon as Ivy sees it, she lets out a moan and tries to scream, but nothing comes out. Turning her around, both Stone and I draw in our breaths at the exact same time. He's torn her back to shreds. Christ, she isn't going to be able to handle any more.

"Okay, Walker, you win. Stone will give you the computer so you can stop hurting her now. Please, I'm begging you, Walker."

He turns to me with a sick grin on his face. "Fuck, Quinn. I have waited ten years for you to beg me again. I almost came in my jeans. Now we're gettin' somewhere. Computer first, then you and I are gonna get reacquainted again. Stone, I see you don't like that idea, but I don't give a flying fuck. You've been a pain in my ass for years, and it stops today, so step up and give the bag to

Quinn, or I'll shoot you both. I have no issues of using your friend here as a shield if you get the itch to shoot, Stone. You'll bring that bag to me, Quinn, and then we're leaving. This is the only way this ends. Otherwise, you'll continue to live on the run from me for the rest of your life, or you'll die, right along with Viola and Raven."

I stare at him and know now is the time to reveal my secret. I would never leave my children, no matter who or what is at risk.

"Walker, I can't do that … not yet, anyway. You might not know this, but it's hard to believe since you seem to find everything out. I can't leave Cari and Benjamin, no matter what, and before you ask, they are our children."

Watching the shock consume his features, I continue, "Yeah, that's right, asshole. That night, the only good that came from it was my children—*my* twin children, and I refuse to leave them, so you need to come up with another plan."

CHAPTER 25

Watching Walker's face as Quinn tells him about the kids, I realize she's buying us some time. Damn, this woman thinks on her feet better than some of my associates. Knowing we don't have a lot of time, I set my own plan in motion.

"Walker, I'll give you the computer and in place of Quinn, you can take me." Quinn's head jerks around as Walker stares at me with that evil grin.

"Why the fuck would I take you instead of her? We can pick up the brats and be on our way in no time at all. You have nothing I want except that bag, so don't even think about it, Stone."

"Well, I think you'll change your mind when I tell you that we know your father's partners have taken a hit out on you. Your time is limited, Walker, so why drag Quinn and two innocent kids into it? You and me go way back, so maybe I can help you get out of the country, avoid this hit, and start somewhere fresh with no history. You took care of Jazz Man, and no one's seen or heard from Mario, so there are no loose ends."

I can see he's thinking hard about my idea. Looking at Quinn, I cringe at the look on her face. She looks devastated, and I have no idea why. She mouths, "You aren't doing this," and I get it. She doesn't want me to go with him. I give her my cocky smile and a wink. Little does she know I've had this idea for a while, but wasn't sure how I would get him alone without Quinn or anyone else around. I always knew it would be the two of us, and only one would be walking away. I can't chance him getting away and continuing to haunt Quinn and her sisters.

Knowing I have him, I keep reeling him in.

"Walker, your connections are dried up. You know it, and so do I, but my connections are as hot as ever. Tell me where you want to go, and that will be where you end up. All I want is to walk out of this store, back to my SUV, and leave Quinn, Ivy, and the rest of these folks alone. You've made your point, loud and clear. Let's get out of here before the cops, FBI, and CIA show up. Once they get their hands on you, you're done. I won't be able to help you then."

Watching the indecision on his face, he walks up to Quinn, stopping directly in front of her. I keep my gun trained on him. She stays perfectly still, but I see her body start to tremble. He reaches his hand up, and still Quinn doesn't move. She stares straight at him as he caresses her cheek, then goes into her hair, running his fingers through it. His eyes close for a moment, taking his last moment with her in, then opens them, looking directly into her eyes. "Are the kids really mine, or were you playing me?"

She shakes her hair loose from his fingers so his hand lands on her shoulder.

"Honestly, I don't know which one of you are the father of my children. It doesn't matter because they are *my children*—always have been, always will be. I'd die protecting them. Hear me, Walker? I mean that to my last breath."

He continues to watch her, looking for what, who knows? Finally, he leans in, his lips barely touching her cheek.

"Watch over them carefully, Quinn. There are more of my type than yours out there. Never know whose watching and waiting. For what it's worth, I wish they were mine, but we'll never know, will we? Goodbye, dear Quinn."

He looks to me and nods. I keep a tight hold on the bag over my shoulder, and as I pass Quinn, she grabs my hand, holding on tight.

"Please, Stone, don't go. There's no need for you to go to this extreme. Think about your life. It'll change forever if you do this. I need you, the twins need you, and so does your crew. Stone, you're our rock."

Watching her finally open up, tears me to pieces. Why now, after all this time? She has no idea that I got this, and I can't let on because I need the upper hand with Walker.

"Sugar, you know I'll always make sure you're safe. No matter what, never forget that. Take care of Cari and Benjamin. Tell them I love them. Get Ivy some help and let Johnny help with whatever you need. You know how I feel, Quinn, you've known for a while. You're here." I pound my chest then without another word, turn and follow Walker out the front door.

Sitting in the hospital room with Ivy, I know what Stone did was the only option. Both Johnny and Diesel tried to break it down for me, and even though I get it, I'm pissed beyond all reason. We were just getting to know each other, and all the aggression I had for him was gone. He'd awoken feelings in me that have been dead for ten years.

Looking at my best friend, I know we have a long road ahead of us to get her back. The physicians told us that we're lucky she's still alive. They put her in a medically induced coma due to the pain level, and wanted to give her body a break. Johnny never wanders too far, and from the intense look in his eyes, I get the feeling he is going to be around to give her a hand in her recovery anyway he can.

Jimmy and Dorothy are also being treated and will make full recoveries. I called Raven to inform her and Viola about what happened. They were both shocked about Stone going with Walker—stunned, actually.

Sitting with my head in my hands, trying to come to grips with everything that's happened, I'm beyond shocked.

How do I go on from here? Everything we talked about, Stone and I, about our future with the kids, I can't even think about it now. He left me to save our lives, but what kind of life is it without him? I'm finally able to let go of all my baggage and truly open up for the first time and for what? So he could just up and leave me? I have no idea what to do or where to go. Stone and I had been working on our friendship first before we decided to go any further, but now I'm alone yet again, and hate the feeling. I've come to depend on him to make me feel again, laugh, hold me when I cried, and just be there for me.

I'm lost again, because of Stone.

CHAPTER 26

Not sure what the fuck happened. As I rub my hands through my hair, I feel like someone has beaten the fucking shit out of me. It hurts to raise my arms up, and even worse, when I take a breath. Trying to open my eyes, which feel like they're swollen shut, I attempt to shift around, only to realize that I'm lying on some type of flooring in a very dark room. The only light coming in is from a small window with bars up high on the far wall.

Finally able to pry my eyes open, I try to clear the shit out and look around; not much to see. It looks like a bare prison cell. Squinting, I glance around and see something across from me—something or someone is lying with their body away from me so all I see is their back. They're curled into a ball and not moving. What the fuck is going on and who the fuck is it?

I try to remember what happened and it hits me. I left with Walker from Quinn's bakery and we got into his Range Rover. After that, I don't remember much of anything. How is that possible? Did he drug me? Where am I, and why?

Just as my mind is playing catch up, I hear a key opening a lock. I try to see who's coming in, but all I can do is smell food. My stomach jerks like crazy, and I realize that I'm starving. Next, I look up and I'm shocked at who's carrying in the tray.

"Son-of-a-bitch! Marco, what the fuck is going on, and why am I in here? Where's that motherfucker, Walker?"

"Calm down, Stone, just calm the hell down. Take a deep breath and let me put this shit down."

He carefully walks to me, gesturing for me to take the tray. Grabbing it with both hands, I'm surprised at how heavy it is until I bring it down and see my Glock sitting on it with some food. I'm confused.

"Drink the coffee, Stone. You're going to need it. I'll fill you in, just give me a moment to move this piece of shit out of here."

He goes to the curled up body and grabs the person's arm, pulling him straight, then drags him out of the room. I hear the chains before I see he's shackled, hands and legs together. When I get a glimpse of his face, I feel immediate disgust and hatred run through my veins. It's Walker, and he looks like he's almost dead.

"Hang on, Marco. Wait a fuckin' minute. Why isn't that asshole dead and getting colder by the minute?"

Calling out, I see two men approach Marco and each take one of Walker's arms, dragging him across to a separate room and throwing him in, not too gracefully, and locking the door. Marco turns and enters my room, squatting down against the wall.

Taking a deep breath to calm myself, I count to twenty and start.

"So, did he ever find out that you actually worked for me, Marco? Is that why you were on the run and your family disappeared? Did you report in to the Bureau, letting them know the status of the case?"

"Hang on, Stone. All in good time, buddy. No, he didn't find out I worked on your team until he brought you here and I was waiting on both of you. He was confused at first, but when the guys came out in their fucking jackets, screaming DEA, CIA and FBI, he figured it out and went nuts. Took five guys to contain him, and then I laid into him, something I've wanted to do for so fucking long. Well, I did what you wished you could have. His face looks like ground meat and it felt fuckin' good to do it. That motherfucker ruined my life and I needed to give it back to him. Now, to answer your question, the *'company'* wants Walker alive so they can retrieve all the product and cash he's got stashed away. Those are my orders from the top brass. So, buddy, that's what I'm doing. I'm going to turn Walker in and then disappear. Have the family already gone, and I mean gone. No one will ever find us when this is over. That was always my plan, Stone. Since that night with Quinn and her family, I've gone along with whatever anyone wanted, but now my family comes first. For fuck's sake, dude, I have kids. I can't let anything happen to them, ever."

Marco takes a much-needed breath, then continues.

"I know that night ten years ago was fucked up ... and poor Quinn. I don't know how she survived, but she did. Damn, that chick is one strong woman. I've never gotten over that night. I raped an innocent woman, and no matter the circumstances, I shouldn't have done it. First and last time for that. I'll never be able to forgive myself for that, but what I can do is what you and I worked for these last ten years. To bring Walker down, and dude, we did it. He's going to pay for everything he did. One way or another, he's going to pay."

I listen to everything Marco is sharing with me. No one knew, not even Diesel or Johnny that Marco was on the same team with me when Quinn's family was destroyed. He was doing a job, and we were both fucked over. He was the inside man and played a part he never should've had to play. Since then, he's been one of us. It had to be kept quiet and confidential. The only reason Spirit knew was because over the years, she's fixed up Marco from some of the sick shit Walker's pulled. I'm talkin' really fucked up, pyscho shit.

"So, what you're telling me is that we worked all this time to bring that piece of shit down and now 'they' decide they need information from him. He gets to live? That's fucking bullshit, Marco. Do you have any idea how many women and children he's hurt over the years? Of course you do. I can't let there be even a remote chance that he'd be able to escape and come at Quinn and her family again. No fucking way. I want that motherfucker put to ground, Marco. They promised me that. All I ever asked for is that Walker not be left breathing when this was all over. Can you really live with yourself, without looking over your shoulder, knowing that asshole is still drawing a breath? Be honest. Look me in the eyes and tell me you're good with it."

Watching the struggle Marco's going through, I finish it off.

"Marco, buddy, do you want there to be a small chance that Walker could get to your wife or daughters? Cause after all this and you working against him, you know that sadistic bastard will find them and take it out on them to get back at you. Are you really gonna take that chance?"

I know I've got him when he shakes his head, eyes glaring at me.

"Get up, Stone. Let's finish this."

He helps me to my feet and I stumble, trying to get my bearings. I let the last ten years run through my head. I don't just murder people because I can, but in my head, I pull up the photos of what he and his boys did to Quinn, and all the other women who weren't as lucky; the ones he killed, and the young girls he shipped off to rich assholes, wanting their own little playthings to fuck with and torture.

I almost puke at the thought, but I hold it together. Giving Marco a chin lift, letting him know I'm ready, we walk to the room across the hall. Marco screams at his men to bring him the key to open the door. Once it's opened, we're shocked to see Walker standing against the far wall, watching and waiting like a trapped animal. He knows his time has come, and he's trying to figure out a way to avoid the inevitable. Marco walks in the room first, and I follow behind, glaring at my onetime childhood friend turned psychopath.

"Walker, the time has finally come. You'll never hurt another human being again. We can't let it happen, and I don't care what your deal is with the bureau. I had my own deal, and apparently, they don't think they need to honor it, so fuck them. Anything you want to say before I put a bullet through your fucked up brain?"

He laughs, and hearing it sends shivers down my spine.

"You boys might think this is the end, but don't bet on it. You might be able to take me down, but that doesn't eliminate the people I work for. You know my dad's empire. They'll come at you one at a time, and it won't be pretty, I can promise you that."

I let out a growl then a small laugh.

"Asshole, you have no idea. That "empire" you speak about is already gone. We took it apart three days ago, and most are either dead or in jail. So, keep thinking that you'll have your revenge, but honestly, you're only going to become food for maggots and worms."

He thinks for a minute, then lunges towards us. All you hear are the bullets being released from our guns. My first bullet hits him right between the eyes, and I watch as the back of his head bursts open, brains splattering against the wall behind him. By the time he hits the ground, he's torn to shreds from the amount of bullets we've fired at him. I actually drop to the ground as it all finally comes to an end. Ten years of hard ass grinding work, and this is it. Walker is dead. More importantly, Quinn is safe. No more worries for her, her children, or her sisters.

For a brief second I feel bad for the childhood friend I thought I knew, but that fleeting empathy is gone as quickly as it came. He doesn't deserve anything. He actually got what was coming to him.

Turning to Marco, I see he has a huge grin on his face.

"Dude, did ya see him fall to pieces, and I mean literally? God, that felt so fucking good, didn't it, Stone? It's finally over … finally."

I reach out to him and give him a sideways hug.

"Marco, thanks for all you've done. I wish you and yours only the best. Try to stay in touch, but if ya can't, I get it. Before you take off, stop by and say goodbye to both Quinn and myself."

"Stone, you know Quinn will not want to see me anywhere near her, but I appreciate the sentiment. Let me clean this shit up while you go and get back to her.

She's probably a wreck, not knowing what's going on."

I look into his eyes and see the pain, regret, and the sorrow he still carries, but I also see a new light—a light of forgiveness and love for his part in all of Quinn's pain.

Shaking his hand, I turn to leave and hear his words, "You know what, dude? You're way too lucky. "

"Don't I know it?"

As I'm driving back to our town, I reflect on so many things. First and foremost are Quinn and her family. They're safe for the first time in ten long years. Then I think of my crew. We've busted our asses to bring this asshole down. We were consumed with it and let it take over our lives. Then my thoughts move to Ivy, who will have a long recovery, but she also made it out alive. There are always casualties in any war, and this was a war with Walker. But knowing that everyone has a future makes it bearable.

I know that all of us involved will move forward to whatever the future holds without regrets. Where we all end up is gonna be our choice. It is up to each of us to determine what our futures can be, as life has no limits now.

We have dealt with the past and the ANGUISH, and the present with a VENGEANCE. The future is an AWAKENING, and I can't wait to embrace my future with Quinn, Benjamin, and Cari.

I just pray Quinn feels the same way. The future will tell.

THANK YOU

My heartfelt thanks for your purchase of VENGEANCE. I truly hope you enjoyed Book Two in The Journals Trilogy.

If you did, please take a moment to leave a short honest review on the purchase site. Each review means the world to me as it comes from you the reader. Also your reviews assist me in promoting my name and books to new readers.

AWAKENING is the final book in this Trilogy. Get ready for the ride of your life.

ABOUT THE AUTHOR

D. M. Earl resides in Northwest Indiana. An avid reader since childhood she has taken the next steps to start writing professionally. When not reading or writing D.M. can be found on her 04 Harley hitting the road beside her husband riding his own 2011 Harley. She also enjoys being outdoors gardening or working in one of her many flowerbeds. An avid pet lover D.M. can be found on her back deck with her two pits laying at her feet enjoying the sun and chimes as the indoor cats look out. There are also multiple strays living in their garage and her & her husband feed the wildlife in the area.

If you would like to contact me, please do so at dmearl14@gmail.com, or by snail mail:

D. M. Earl
P.O. Box 306
Dyer, Indiana 46311

Below are my social media links to stay in contact and hear about all my works in progress and upcoming releases. You can find me on Facebook, Amazon, Twitter, TSU, and Goodreads.

Facebook (Like) http://bit.ly/dmearl14

Amazon **http://bit.ly/amazondmearl**

Twitter **http://bit.ly/twitterdmearl**

TSU **http://bit.ly/tsudmearl**

Goodreads **http://bit.ly/goodreadsdmearl**

I'm also including my newsletter and website in case you would like to sign up for updates on a monthly basis.

Newsletter-
http://bit.ly/newsletterdmearl
Website https://dmearl.com

WHEELS & HOGS SERIES

Connelly's Horde

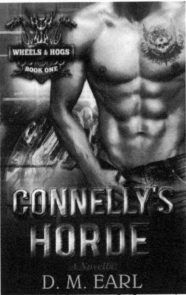

Welcome to Desmond Connelly's Horde or better known as his extended family at Wheels & Hogs Garage. For years these survivors have been dealing with what life throws them while trying to move forward from the atrocities in their lives. Some have secrets not shared while others are working through problems that are continually present in their lives.

Follow Des as he introduces you to each one of his crew at Wheels & Hogs in this short Novella. Start to understand how a group of strangers become not only friends but family over the years. Get a snapshot of why when life pushes you down, in this garage, you push back until you are on your feet again.

Connelly's Horde
http://amzn.to/1DNnMD5

Cadence Powers is tattooed, pierced, and panty dropping gorgeous. Women love him and men want to be him. It appears to the world that he has it all, but what people don't see is that Cadence is a damaged haunted man, held back by untold secrets that keep him from living a real life.

When he meets Trinity Vinkers, he feels as if he can finally live the life he desperately wants. However, just as their friendship begins to grow, one stupid act causes that friendship to shatter, all because he lets his guard down allowing her into his life.

Trinity appears to be the light to Cadence's dark. Innocent, naïve, and goofy, she seems to bring out the best in everyone around her, but she has her own dark secret. Her persona allows her to fake her way through life, at least until she meets him. Trying not to let her feelings for Cadence get the best of her is taken out of her hands when she makes a wrong decision that leaves her left with an unexpected fallout.

As life takes both Cadence and Trinity down a

path that neither will forget, they are unaware of the evil lurking around them. It's watching, waiting to step in and take everything from Cadence.

As the young lovers struggle with their secrets, a close friend will also be fighting for something,... her life. As time goes by, Cadence and the Horde from Wheels & Hogs decide that they have to do whatever it takes to keep what is theirs safe, even as death hovers around like a dark angel.

Cadence Reflection
http://bit.ly/CadenceDMEarl

Gabriel "Doc" Murphy found the woman he'd planned to treasure for the rest of his life in a young, shy girl he had seen being bullied in a hallway between classes when they were just kids. Over the years, Doc loved and protected her with all he had, until the day came when he received news that there was something that could take her away from him...Cancer. Being faced with the possibility of losing the love of his life, Doc would turn the world inside-out to save and keep the only love that could shatter him, body and soul, if he couldn't save her.

Fern knew the instant she fell into Gabriel's arms all those years ago, that she had found her "one and only." He became her everything-owning her heart and soul. As they made it through their life journey together, nothing could tear their unbreakable bond. Life struggles, financial losses, and even devastating miscarriages didn't stand a chance until the day she received the phone call that finally shattered their world to the core, leaving Fern preparing for the fight of her life.

As Doc and Fern struggle through each day, praying for a miracle, one presents itself. Do they dare have hope, or do they accept that the fight is over as a dark shadow waits patiently to make a move to alter their lives forever.

Gabriel's Treasure
http://bit.ly/GabrielDMEarl

JOURNALS TRILOGY

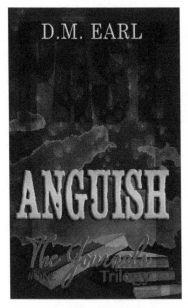

My name is Quinn and in one night my life changed forever. I lost not only part of my family, but also a huge part of who I was. Struggling to make it through each dark day, uncertain of everything in my life, I'm barely living just existing until a professional suggests I start writing down my thoughts in a journal.

My journals help me muddle through the personal and emotional baggage. Allow me to manage the past with all my Anguish; to function in the present plotting Vengeance; and to hope for my Awakening to a future full of all my dreams for a better life.

That is, until my past comes full force into my present and threatens my future. And the only person who can help me is someone from my past. The same person who has been around in the shadows protecting me, even when I didn't know he was there, apparently has always had my back.

Anguish
http://bit.ly/AnguishDMEarl